CHARLOTTE PATEL

PLAY THERAPY

⭐ Activities ⭐

150 FUN ACTIVITIES FOR PARENTS AND CHILDREN TO PLAY TO IMPROVE EMOTIONAL STABILITY AND BONDING

Contents

The Aim & Objectives of the Book

Play Therapy is an evidence-based practice for children who suffer from trauma and family dysfunction. It is designed to help parents and children become more familiar with the concepts and develop an understanding of what play therapy is, how it works, and can help. It has activities for parents and children to work on to develop further play therapy knowledge and how it can help.

Playing is a natural part of the human experience. The ever-expanding definition of playing got a new meaning recently when the United Nations issued a report stating that children have the right to have fun. That's why you'll find activities for parents and children in this book to promote emotional stability and bonding. Play Therapy Activity Book is a 45-minute-long book with activities for parents and children to play.

Many parents are discovering the benefits of playing with their children. Research has shown that playing with children is a great way to provide emotional support and intimacy and develop a strong bond between parents and children. Play therapy is a form of therapy that uses games and play in a way that can improve emotional, cognitive, behavioral, and social functioning. Play therapy is recommended for children struggling with developmental delays and learning disabilities. It includes activities that help children develop the necessary cognitive life skills.

Who Should Read This Book?

Everyone should read this book. In this book, you will find activities for parents and children to play and promote emotional stability and bonding. The reader should be of a certain age but not be required to be a parent or a child. The book is intended for professionals who work with children and parents. If you are just a parent, it is not a requirement that you have played the activities in the book with your children. It should be read by those who work with children, not those who work with parents.

With this book, you will have a lot of fun while you bring out your child's inner mind. Play Therapy stimulates kids' brains in ways similar to what is done in a traditional therapy session. The book offers simple ideas for parents and their children to play together, promoting emotional stability and bonding. Who should read this book?

Parental anxiety is the state that occurs when parents experience a change in behavior in their children. It is a natural state of being, brought on by the natural evolution of a parent's role as a caregiver. When children are born, a new type of love takes place. The parent bonds with the baby and pampers the child, developing a sense of love, care, and nurturing that is pure and authentic. It is a love that is not based on the child's best behavior or performance but the parent's love for the child.

INTRODUCTION

If a youngster does not have the tools to express themselves, they may turn to unhealthy outlets. It can lead to attachment issues and emotional instability. It will look at some activities you can do with your child to promote emotional stability.

Play therapy is a growing field that's relied on by many therapists. It's often used when children are struggling with issues in their life. It is because play is a therapeutic activity that allows children to express different emotions and bond with their parents. It has play activities for parents and children to promote emotional stability and bonding.

This book looks at play therapy's importance in children's lives. We examine different ideas for games and activities for parents and children to play that can promote emotional stability and bonding. When children are stimulated and allowed to express their thoughts safely and creatively, they can develop more positive feelings, leading to a better life.

Play is an important part of growing up and helps children learn important skills. It allows them to express themselves and practice contributing to the family unit. Activities like playing games, playing, and coloring is all-natural ways to help children build emotional stability and bonding. It will look at the play therapy activity book and how you can use it to help your child build confidence, form healthy emotional habits and get closer to you.

Playing with a child is a way to break the ice and connect. Playtime can be a fun way for a child to overcome their negative emotions and be able to work through their difficulties. However, playtime can be very difficult if someone feels a lot of distress or stress. It will discuss how you can use a play therapy activity book to help your child overcome their difficulties.

Play Therapy is a type of therapy through which a child can express emotions or encounter various situations they would not be able to do in real life. It will look at the various activities you can use in your Play Therapy session.

Chapter 1: How to Break Your Kid of Screen Addiction and Keep Them Healthy and Happy

Screen addiction is one of the biggest challenges parents faces. It's hard to break your kid of screen addiction, but there are a few things you can do to help. First, it's significant to get them used to screens in general, not just their computer screen. Second, set goals for how much time they spend on screens each day, and WEEKLY! And finally, make sure they have healthy activities outside of screens (like books, music, etc.) that keep them active and engaged.

How to Break Your Kid of Screen Addiction.

One of the most common screen addiction problems is children's screen addiction. It can be a problem because screens can be very addicting and have negative consequences for you and your child.

There are a few ways to break your child of their screen addiction:

1. Talk to them about screens and how they impact their lives. Screen addiction can cause problems for you and your child by leading them away from real-life experiences. By talking about screens and how they impact their lives, you'll help them understand why they need to stay away from screens to maintain healthy emotional relationships.

2. Get them involved in physical activities or learning outside the screen. Kids must get involved in activities that don't involve screens – this will help keep them occupied, engaged, and healthy overall.

3. Encourage creative expression onscreen and offscreen. Some kids find creative expression onscreen more fun than others, but you must support this type of expression by providing opportunities for it both onscreen and off-screen (i.e., through art, writing, music, etc.).

Some common triggers for screen addiction include watching screens too often or excessively, watching screens for hours on end, using screens as part of daily activities, overindulging in online gaming, and obsessing over screens. It's important to find ways to limit or break these habits so that your child can remain healthy and happy while using screens.

For example, children who spend excessive amounts of time on screens at home may start developing video game skills that could lead them down a path towards professional gaming careers or other forms of competitive entertainment. Additionally, kids constantly exposed to digital violence may develop violent tendencies in adulthood.

Many helpful tips are available to keep your children healthy and happy while using screens. In addition to these tips, you may consider using playtime apps that allow parents access to controlled content when their children are not working or playing onscreen.

How to overcome screen Addiction.

Screen addiction is a common problem that can stop kids from enjoying life. To break screen addiction, you need to understand it and try different strategies to keep your child healthy and happy.

One way to overcome screen addiction is by using screens for different purposes. For example, you can use screens for homework instead of textbooks or for creative activities instead of watching TV or playing video games. You can also set bounds on how often screens are used and ensure that screens are used when needed and positively.

It will help your child develop better focus and concentration, which will help them stay healthy and happy while they watch screens.

How to Prevent Screen Addiction.

It can be difficult to break your child from screen addiction. However, there are a few things you can do to help:

1. Talk to them about their screens and how they impact their lives. It will help them see the extent to which screens are affecting their day-to-day lives.

2. Show them how screen addiction is ruining their health and happiness. Explain that using screens excessively will cause them problems with focus, concentration, and sleep quality, making it hard for them to stay away from screens for long periods.

3. Offer support systems for them – family, friends, or therapists – who can offer guidance on overcoming screen addiction and keeping their children healthy and happy.

Have a Family Conference to Make a Plan of Action

If your child is addicted to screens, it may be time for a family meeting to create an action plan. The meeting will help determine the best way to break the addiction and keep your child healthy and happy. The meeting should include all family members, including parents, children, and grandparents. Everyone must be on the same page when it comes to this issue. If there are disagreements or differences, they will need to be resolved for the whole family to succeed.

Plan for a Day to Initiate Rehabilitation

If your child has been addicted to screens for a while, there is a good chance that they have also developed screen-related addictions in other parts of their life. It aims to provide helpful tips on breaking addiction and keeping them healthy and happy.

Let Them Know About Their Addiction

It can be difficult to break a child of screen addiction from using screens regularly. However, some methods work well for most kids. It will help if you start by telling them about the addiction to understand what's happening and why it's important for them to stay away from screens. It will help them develop better self-esteem and identify any problems with screen use outside of their addiction.

Set Limits on Screen Use

One way to help break your child of screen addiction is by setting limits on onscreen use. If they have unlimited time each day to use screens, it will be difficult for them to break out of their screen habit completely. Instead, set specific times during the day when screens are not allowed and try to stick to these rules consistently. It will help your child develop healthier habits around screens and avoid rebound compulsion or addictive behavior.

Seek Help from a Professional

If your child is having difficulties breaking their screen addiction, seeking professional help may be helpful. A therapist can deliver leadership and provision as you work to break the addiction and keep your child healthy and happy. It could include helping you develop better coping mechanisms, assisting with communication and problem solving and coaching them on managing their screen use healthily.

Help Your Kids Play

Screen addiction is a huge issue for parents, and many ways to help prevent it. Having a family meeting to create a plan of action, helping your kids play outdoors, and creating a rehabilitation plan is important to have a day in which you can begin rehabilitating your kids.

Chapter 2: Restrengthen Bonds with Your Kids

It's important to understand how toddler bonding works. Toddlers are fascinating creatures, and their development is rapid. You may not know everything about them, but you should at least attempt to understand what factors influence the development of a bond between parent and child. In this chapter, we will explore five different aspects that can influence the development of a divine bond between parents and children:

What is the Divine Bond?

The Divine Bonding Process is the process by which two people become friends and share a common bond. The process begins with understanding what the couple wants and needs in life. Once this understanding is reached, they begin to develop mutual respect. From here, it's up to the couple to work together to build a strong divine bond.

What are the Benefits of the Divine Bonding Process

The benefits of a strong divine bond include:

- Better communication

- Decreased stress levels

- Improved relationship skills

- More harmonious home life

- A deeper connection with the divine

What Are the Steps to building a Divine Bond with Your Child

The steps to building a strong divine bond with your child include:

- Understanding each other's needs

- Developing a mutual respect

- Working together to build a strong divine bond

- Deepening the connection

How to Build a Divine Bond with Your Child.

Before you build a divine bond with your child, you must know what type of relationship you want. It will help you set boundaries for the relationship and ensure that it aligns with your spiritual beliefs and values.

Learn About the Divine Bonding Process

The divine bonding process begins with understanding your child better. By doing this, you can create a foundation for a healthy, happy relationship. It would assist if you were also ready to communicate your feelings and opinions openly and honestly, so your child can learn from you.

Get to Know Your Child Better

Getting to know your child better before starting the divine bonding process is important. Responsibility will help you grow a deeper connection with them and help prevent any misunderstandings or hurt feelings during the relationship. Finally, ensure that you are living according to your spiritual beliefs and values when interacting with your child – this will help build a divine bond between you two.

Tips for building a Divine Bond with Your Child.

When building a divine bond with your child, be gentle and compassionate. Avoid making negative comments or judgments about them, and support them in every way possible. It will help create a strong connection between you two and help build a strong relationship that will last throughout their lives.

Avoid Negative Words

Be sure to use only positive words when referring to your child. Instead of using phrases such as "you're such a scruffy little dog," try phrases like "You are so beautiful" or "I love you so much." It will help create an environment where your child can feel loved and supported by both of you.

Be an Optimistic Power in Your Child's Life

Set an instance for your child by existence kind and helpful around others, even if it means taking on some extra work at home or leading by example when it comes to good behavior. Thelwell help encourages other children to mimic what you do, setting an excellent example themselves while growing up.

Building a Divine Bond with your child is one of the most important things you can do for your future. By learning about the process and setting boundaries for a relationship, you will ensure that your bond is strong and lasting. You can help build a loving and successful relationship with your child with helpful tips and advice from this chapter.

Chapter 3: Best Ways to Help Young Kids Develop Self-Control, Concentration, Emotion Management, And Strengthen the Parent-Child Connection

It's not about giving up your life for a few hours each day, and it's about giving up your life for the betterment of others. That's what young kids do when they put their trust in adults. And that's what we want our parents to do, too. We want them to set an example for their children and provide the critical groundwork for healthy self-control, concentration, emotion management, and parent-child relationships. If you help young kids develop these skills daily, you will have a powerful impact on their lives and those around them.

What is self-control?
Self-control is the ability to control one's emotions and behavior. It comes from knowing when to give in and when to take a stand. Children must learn self-control to stay safe, healthy, and happy on their behalf and with their parents.

What are Some Types of Self-Control Activities
Some self-control activities include staying calm under pressure, keeping your mouth shut when you get mad, not giving into temptation, and setting boundaries with your friends and family.

What are Some Types of Emotion Management Activities
Emotional management activities include managing your anger, controlling your stress levels, communicating effectively, reflecting on your feelings, and taking care of yourself physically and emotionally.

What are Some Types of Parent-Child Connection Activities
Parent-child connection activities include talking about weather conditions while driving or flying, singing together while walking or playing together at home, making new friends while traveling,

cooking together while traveling, and spending time together during weeks without school or work (known as "parent bonding time").

How to Help Young Kids Develop Self-Control, Concentration, Emotion Management, and the Parent-Child Connection.

One of the most important things parents can do for their children is to encourage them to develop self-control. It means allowing them to do their thing without having to answer to anyone else. They can ask a parent or guardian for assistance if they feel like they need help with something.

Next, parents must teach their kids how to do their things. It means teaching them to make choices and take responsibility for their actions. For example, if they want to go on a walk with friends but don't have any money saved up, they should be able to ask a parent or guardian for money so they can buy some snacks and head out.

Keep Them safe and healthy

In addition, parents must keep their children safe and healthy while on vacation. They should provide good food and drinks, enough rest (including napping during long trips), and accurate information about health risks for young kids to stay safe online and off the beaten path. Additionally, it's helpful for parents to keep track of what activities their children are involved in so that they can get an idea of where their concentration might be weakest or where there may be potential problems during travel.

Help Them Deal with Difficult Times

If there are difficult times during the trip – such as when one child starts getting sick – parents must help them manage those times by providing support and guidance through difficult conversations or situations. For example, instead of telling them this is how it will always be "okay" when something goes wrong, parents could talk about why this might happen and offer solutions like taking breaks or communicating with other family members who are also vacationing nearby (or even staying at home).

Tips for Helping Young Kids Develop Self-Control, Concentration, Emotion Management, and the Parent-Child Connection.

Let Them Do Their Things

When it comes to toddlers, it's always a good idea to let them do what they want. Just be sure that they are safe and healthy when doing so. Help them deal with difficult times by providing support and guidance and leaving room for freedom and independence.

Keep Them safe and healthy

Your children must be safe when on vacation, especially if they are new to travel. Make sure to keep them watered and fed, provide safe, fun activities to participate in (like roller skating or hiking), and stay close enough to monitor their health status – but far sufficient absent not to be a threat.

Help Them Deal with Difficult Times

When it comes time for family members or friends to deal with difficult family situations, it can be tough for toddlers – especially if they are already struggling with emotions like frustration or fear. You may need to step in as a support system and offer calming words or instructions while also providing space for freedom and autonomy.

Establish routines for Kids

A good way to help children develop self-control, concentration, emotion management, and the parent-child connection is by setting up a routine. It could include setting rules for when they are allowed to play, going to bed/waking up together, eating meals together, playing outside together, and so on. A good way to ensure these routines are established and followed is by using a Parenting Planner.

Teach Kids Anger Management Skills

Anger is a common emotion that can harm parents and children. To help young kids manage anger, parents need to understand the different types of anger, how to identify when it's being expressed, and how to deal with it.

In addition, parents need to provide positive reinforcement for children who are managing anger well. Positive reinforcement helps children handle their anger healthily, which will help them develop self-control and concentration skills. This type of reinforcement also helps improve the parent-child connection.

Create a Reward System for Kids

To help young kids develop self-control, concentration, emotion management, and the parent-child connection, you'll need some basic practice with self-control. Some tips for helping young kids develop these skills include celebrating each day, letting them do their things, teaching them how to do them, and setting up positive routines. Once they've learned how to control their emotions and manage difficult situations, they can establish routines that will keep them happy and productive. By teaching kids anger management skills and creating a reward system for them, you'll be able to provide a fun environment that encourages the development of these important life skills.

Chapter 4: Benefits of Play Therapy for Kids

Play therapy is a countless method to help children with autism. It can increase socialization, communication, and behavior. Play therapy has many benefits, and finding the right program for your child is important. You can research play therapy programs online or in person. Most play therapists have websites where you can read reviews and learn more about the different types of play therapy offered.

Play therapy is a type of mental health care that helps children and adults learn new skills and improve their emotional well-being. Play therapy can help children to relax, develop problem-solving skills, reduce stress, build self-confidence, and increase communication.

Play therapy can be delivered in a variety of ways, including individualized treatment plans (IPT), family play therapy (FPT), group play therapy (GPT), or combination therapies. IPT is the most common play therapy type, typically lasting for about 60 minutes per session. FPT is designed for groups of 10 to 20 children and typically lasts about 2 hours. GPT combines IPT and FPT, typically lasting for about 30 minutes per session. GPT can be used to treat problems such as fear, aggression, anxiety, social isolation, depression, etc.

What are the Advantages of Play Therapy for Children

There are many benefits to playing with children – from improving socialization skills to reducing stress – but here are some of the most commonly cited:

1) Playing is beneficial in terms of cognitive development; better problem-solving skills; reduced anxiety; improved communication ability; increased self-esteem

2) Play therapy has also been shown to help decrease acted-out behaviors such as oppositional defiant disorder (ODD); attention deficit hyperactivity disorder (ADHD); erased negative thoughts; improving sleep quality

3) play therapist training can provide individuals with an additional income stream while providing therapeutic services

4) Play therapy has also been shown to improve school performance, including reading, math, science, and social studies scores

5) A study published in "Play" found that children who had played with others as infants were more likely to have later successful lives than those who did not play

6) In a study published in "The Journal of Experimental Psychology" kids who spent more time playing showed better problem-solving skills and better communication abilities than control kids who did not play

7) A study published in "The Journal of Mental Health" found that children who play with others have lower rates of anxiety, depression, and social isolation than those who do not play

8) In a study published in "The Journal of Experimental Psychology" children who played with others were more confident and less anxious when they finished their tasks than their control group counterparts

How to Make the Most of Play Therapy.

Play therapy can be a great way to help children learn and develop skills. However, it's important to choose the right sessions for your child. Which play therapies are best suited for your child? Here are some tips to get started:

-Depict stories or images that are calming and positive.

-Help children learn about their emotions by playing games and dealing with them.

-Encourage them to communicate their feelings in different ways – through conversation, storytelling, or drawings.

-Make sure play therapy is scheduled in a safe environment.

Set Up Play Therapy Hours

To maximize the benefits of play therapy, set up regular times for it in your home or office. It means setting aside at least two hours each day for play therapy, so you have time to reduce and devote time to your child. Additionally, ensure play therapy is conducted in a quiet environment, so children don't feel rushed or disturbed. Finally, remember that children who are better at communication than others may benefit from more therapy sessions, so be prepared to work with different children accordingly!

Find Play Therapy Games and Activities

If you want to find fun and creative activities for your child while they receive play therapy, try out some games and activities like these:

-Find a game where players must guide a character through an obstacle course using Only One Foot (or another similar game).

-Play catch and other simple games like memory cards or dart boards; these can be liked by both kids and grownups alike!

-Make use of props such as towers or cars; these can be used as part of puzzles or challenges players must complete winning the game.

What to Expect When You Start Play Therapy.

Before starting play therapy, finding the right session for your child is important. There are many different play therapy types, each with its benefits and drawbacks. You'll need to assess their strengths and weaknesses to find the right session for your child. For example, if your child is generally good at problem-solving but struggles with new tasks or activities, they may need more time or guidance in their play sessions.

Find the Games and Activities that Are Right for Your Child

When choosing games and activities for your child, it's important to consider their age and development level. For example, toddlers typically enjoy simple games like peek-a-boo or cowboys and Indians, while older children can enjoy more complex games like Settlers of Catan or Lord of the Rings: The Fellowship of the Ring.

Institutionalize Play Therapy

Institutionalizing play therapy can have several advantages over traditional home play experiences for kids. First, standardized therapy can provide a structured setting where kids can receive the necessary support as they work on problems from an academic perspective rather than a personal standpoint. Second, standardized therapy may help Kids learn how to coexist with others in a healthy environment without feeling overwhelmed or scared by them. Finally, standardized therapy can help kids develop problem-solving skills in a safe and controlled environment.

Play Therapy can have a profound impact on the lives of children. By choosing the right sessions, setting up playtime hours, and institutionalizing play therapy, you can help your child experience positive reinforcement and lasting change. You can help your child become self-sufficient and learn important life skills with the right games and activities.

Chapter 5: How to Build Social Skills for Kids Through Art Therapy

Art therapy is a great way to help kids learn social skills. It can also help improve communication, teamwork, and problem-solving skills. Many different art therapy programs work best for your community. To find the right program for your child, you must research. You can use this guide to find the right art therapist in your area.

What is Art Therapy?

Art therapy is a type of mental health care focusing on healing. It can help children and adults develop social skills, communication, self-esteem, and more.

There are many types of art therapy available, including:

1) Painting: Painters' paintings may explore different aspects of emotions and experiences, such as joy, sorrow, love, and anger.

2) Sculpting: This form of art therapy can be used to explore different levels of creativity and productivity.

3) Drawing: Drawing can explore feelings such as joy, sadness, anxiety, or anger.

How to Use Art Therapy.

When working with children, choosing the right art therapy material is important. It can include paintings, drawings, sculptures, or any other medium that can be used to express oneself. Though, it's also significant to select the right technique; for example, choosing a method that is easy for your child to understand and follow.

Choose the Right Technique

Once you have chosen the right art therapy material and technique, it's time to start practicing! It's helpful to find an artist who you feel comfortable working with and whose work you enjoy. To help your child learn how to express themselves through art, it helps to practice with them in a safe and controlled environment.

Learn About the Different Types of Art Therapy

Different types of art therapy can be effective for different kids. For example, physical therapy may be used on children with physical problems such as arthritis or a chronic medical condition. Mental health support may benefit children struggling with emotions like anxiety or depression. And emotionally supportive art therapy may be used on kids struggling with difficult topics like anger or sadness.

Practice Art Therapy with Your Kids

When using art therapy with your kids, it's important to practice with them regularly and find a way that they are comfortable with. In addition, it's also important to be clear about the goals of the therapy and what type of results you hope to achieve. By practicing art therapy with your children, you can help them build social skills that will help them feel more linked to the world around them.

Advice for How to Use Art Therapy with Your Kids.

Finding time for art therapy can be difficult, but that doesn't mean you need to give up on it. In fact, by making art therapy fun and engaging for your kids, you may be able to encourage them to make more creative art. For example, try creating a short story or painting contest in which they have to create a masterpiece in an hour or less.

Encourage Your Kids to Make Art

If your kids are struggling with creativity or expression, it may be helpful to encourage them to start making their art. It can include simple things like drawing or painting without preconceptions or ideas about what looks good. Once they start expressing themselves creatively, it will be easier to explore their artistic potential further and improve their technique.

Use Art Therapy to Build Social Skills

Social services are one of the greatest significant services you can develop as a parent. By using art therapy as a tool for boosting these skills, you may be able to help your children develop closer relationships with other people and learn how to interact positively and effectively with others – both in the present and in the future.

Building social-emotional skills with art therapy

Art therapy aims to help children develop social, emotional, and cognitive skills. Art therapy generally helps children process and understand feelings and emotions by using creative expression. It can be used in a traditional or mixed-methods setting.

Art therapy is often used in traditional settings with children struggling with difficult emotions like anger, sadness, and anxiety. Mixed-methods settings utilize traditional and non-traditional methods to help the child process their emotions. Different techniques may be used in this setting, including group therapy, psychoanalysis, sculpting, painting, writing, dance, and psychology/behavioral manipulations.

Art therapy is a real instrument for serving children to develop social skills as well as emotional intelligence. Studies have found that when children can understand how they feel and express themselves through art, they are more likely to feel Supported by Art Therapy Services

Art therapy may be a great option if you're looking for ways to improve your social-emotional skills. You can help your children build their social-emotional skills using the right methods and materials. Additionally, by working with your kids in art therapy, you can help them learn about their feelings and how to connect them effectively. Advice for how to use art therapy with your kids is also included in this document.

Chapter 6: Engage Children Through Conversation and By Asking Questions

A conversation is a discussion of ideas between two people to develop rapport, discover common ground, or exchange information. There has to be a rotation of speakers between the two sides. It's common practice for each person to respond to the other's statement as the discussion progresses. It is common for youngsters to acquire communication conventions by eavesdropping on and then joining in on adult talks.

Even before a child can speak, they may communicate with their environment.

It's never too early to start talking to a kid, even before they can talk back. Children utilize non-verbal cues like looking at one another or making eye contact to start conversations before they can communicate.

Taking a gander at the grownup

indicating a target with one's finger

carrying out a procedure

producing a noise

Parentages should use their finest ruling to figure out what their kid is trying to communicate when they engage in any of these behaviors and then attempt to carry on the discussion using words.

Choose Appropriate Resources

Any readings or discussion starters you use with a child should be suitable for their age group. Ben, age 8, did not engage with his mother while she told him the Sherlock Holmes narrative because he was uninterested. Ben would have listened more attentively if his mother had discussed more age-appropriate themes, such as robots.

Allow the kid to pick out the supplies. Children are more likely to participate in the discussion following a decision they have helped make. You may, for instance, inquire as to whether the kid prefers Legos or toy cars. By focusing the discussion on the item, he chose, you can keep his attention and the conversation going.

Have meaningful conversations with your child while you go about your daily routines.

It's common for people to talk to one another while doing normal things around the house, like cooking or taking a shower. There is no essential for luxurious toys or special materials if parents just chat to their kids about their day as they go about their normal routines. Because John's mother often used the phrase "soap" while in the shower, he eventually picked up on the word and started using it himself.

Be Engaging in Your Speech

Kids love it when grownups use a cheerful voice while interacting with them.

Maintaining Communication

Here are some easy habits to keep the dialogue going with your kid:

If a youngster is talking, pay attention to what they are saying since that is where your focus should be. Just keep talking about whatever it is that your kid is into. Sarah's mother followed her example and began talking about the bird in the artwork rather than continuing the tale when Sarah brought up the topic during story time.

Don't forget to stop after you've finished talking or asking a question to show the youngster that they now have the floor to answer. The silence should be long enough for the kid to formulate a coherent answer.

Children's speech often consists of a few basic words or phrases that they repeatedly repeat and elaborate upon. With your guidance, your child's babbling may grow into whole sentences with the addition of new vocabulary and grammatical structures.

Conversations with kids should be lighthearted and not used as a kind of assessment.

Kids are frustrated when their parents quiz them endlessly to see whether they've retained any of their lessons. Keep the dialogue lighthearted and easy to start or continue with your kid.

Chapter: Fun Activities with Classic Materials

Homemade modeling clay

Especially for smaller kids, getting their hands on some fresh play dough and letting them mold it into anything they can imagine may be both therapeutic and instructive. Young muscles can have fun while developing strength, control, and fine motor abilities with the assistance of these squishy craft supplies. Our simple recipe for play dough is just as wonderful (if not better) and cheaper than whatever you could acquisition in a store, so there's no need to go out and buy any.

Do nothing but babble or claim to be psychic.

It's not essential to be an expert crafter to make our origami chatterbox out of paper and pencil. Its toy is a huge hit with kids, and they'll have a blast playing with it and customizing it with their buddies.

Make a board out of bolts.

A wrench is an essential part of each beginner's initial toolkit. Use the wrenches to fasten the matching-colored nuts to the bolts after the youngsters have helped drill holes of the appropriate size in the boards.

Slides and ball pits: the playground essentials

Especially for smaller kids, I think this is a brilliant idea and a lot of fun. You may find both ball pits and pools for sale on the internet. Then you may fill it with balls and put it on a slide that children will like. Watch your child as they spend hours having fun on the slide. The fun factor is quite high.

A window with a stain on it

No of their age, children would like this plan. But the accompanying lesson has been removed. As seen in the image, cutting tissue paper will have to wait until after a plastic sheet has been hung. The puzzle may be assembled with the help of glue or tape, and your children should be encouraged to utilize it.

Puzzles

As early as the middle of March, it was clear that puzzles would be a desirable commodity. This aim is ideal for people who prefer to work alone or just want quiet time to recharge. It's common for younger kids to plead for assistance before they get it continually. However, if you can make youngsters feel safe figuring things out there and then lavish them with praise, you may foster a more independent personality. We recommend throwing in some 3D puzzles for variety.

A "Color Experiment" full of air bubbles

The rainbow colors may be made by putting baking soda into a deep container and then adding a little food coloring to each muffin cup. Vinegar may be administered to kids using spray bottles or pipettes (baby medicine droppers are ideal for this). At that point, you may stand back and enjoy the "volcano" effect and the thrill of trying out various color combinations.

Disagreements with the question "Where are you?"

A little bit of homework work in advance will pay off here. Put away some of your children's most prized belongings for them to locate at a later time, such as cherished stuffed animals, action figures, or dolls. Encourage imaginative play in your kids by telling them their toys are playing hide-and-seek. They may spend the day looking for their buddies if they haven't found them by the afternoon.

Use a Squirt Gun to Paint

One of our favorite DIY art and craft ideas for kids is spray painting, and it's always a pleasure to do with them. Allow your future Jackson Pollock to shine by creating these stunning works of art. On a warm straw-hat day, the courtyard is the ideal location for a party. Make nightly of it by attracting some pals and neighbors.

Chapter 7: Care through play: Importance for Play for Kids

Play is one of the greatest significant features of a child's life. It helps with their physical, mental, emotional, and social development. Play also helps children learn new skills and understand their world.

Physical benefits
There are many benefits to children playing. It helps them to grow bodily, spiritually, emotionally and socially.

Playing helps children to develop their gross motor skills (using large muscles to move), fine motor skills (using small muscles to do delicate tasks), and coordination (being able to use different body parts together). It also helps them to develop their cardiovascular (heart and lungs) and musculoskeletal (bones and muscles) systems.

Mental benefits
Playing helps children to develop their cognitive skills (thinking, reasoning, problem solving), memory, imagination, and creative thinking. It also helps them to develop their self-control, focus, and attention span.

Emotional benefits
Playing helps children to develop their emotional regulation (ability to manage emotions), empathy (ability to understand and share the emotions of others), and social skills (ability to interact with others). It also helps them to feel happy, confident, and secure.

Social benefits
Playing with others helps children to develop their cooperation, communication, collaboration, and negotiation skills. It also helps them to understand social rules and norms, resolve conflicts peacefully, and build relationships.

Regular play has been shown to have a number of benefits for children, both mental and physical. In terms of mental benefits, play can help children develop their imagination, creativity, and problem-solving skills. Play can also help children develop their social skills by allowing them to interact with other children and learn how to cooperate and share.

In terms of physical benefits, play can help children to develop their gross motor skills (the ability to use large strengths, such as those in the legs and arms) and their fine motorized skills (the ability to use small muscles, such as those in the hands and fingers). Play can also assistance broods to develop their coordination and balance.

As children engage in play, they learn how to interact with other people and develop social skills such as coordination, Sharing, teamwork and leadership. Play also provides a great opportunity for children to learn how to resolve conflict. When children are playing together, they often have to negotiate who gets which role and how the game should be played. It helps them to grow important skills such as endurance, flexibility and empathy.

One of the most important benefits of play is that it helps children to develop their emotions. As they explore different situations and work out how to deal with them, they learn how to control their feelings and fast them appropriately. Play also helps children to understand the emotions of others and to develop empathy.

The importance of play

Children need to play. It is through play that they learn about the world around them. When they play, they are able to explore new things, try out new ideas and make mistakes. All of this is crucial for their learning and development.

For the individual child

Child's play is important for the development of vital life skills. Through play, children learn critical skills like how to think creatively, solve problems, communicate with others, and cope with emotions and stress. Play also helps children develop physical coordination and motor skills.

There are many different types of play, but all of them are important for children's development. exploratory play helps children learn about their environment and try out new things. Imaginative play allows children to express themselves creatively and use their imaginations. Physically active play helps children develop their large and small muscles as well as their coordination. social play gives children a chance to practice interacting with others and develop important social skills.

Each kind of play has its aids, but the most important thing is that children have time to just play without adults interfering too much. It's okay to step in if a child is in danger or needs help; otherwise, it's best to let children figure things out for themselves. It is how they learn best!

For the family

Many experts believe that play is essential for children's development and learning. Play provides children with opportunities to explore, experiment, practice new skills, and try new ideas. It also helps children to develop their imaginations, improve their problem-solving skills and learn how to cooperate with others.

Play is important for children's physical development. It helps them grow their uncultured motor skills (using large muscles to move around) and fine motor skills (using small muscles to pick up objects). Play also helps children to develop their coordination and balance.

Play is also important for children's mental development. Finished play, children learn about themselves and the world around them. They also learn how to cope with emotions, solve problems and deal with disappointment.

Play is important for social development. Through play, children learn how to communicate with others, share, take turns and negotiate. They also learn how to resolve conflicts peacefully.

Finally, play is important for emotional development. Through play, children can express their feelings, work through difficult experiences and develop a positive sense of self-esteem.

For the community

Play is important for children's social skills and their ability to interact with others. Children learn how toward share, take turns, and resolve conflict through play. They also develop a sense of empathy and compassion for others.

Play also helps children develop their imaginations, learn to problem solve, and think creatively. When children engage in open-ended play, they can try out new ideas, experiment with different solutions, and use their imaginations.

Play is a significant part of child growth and has been linked to improved academic performance, increased creativity, reduced stress levels, and even happier adults. Play is not just for children – it is good for businesses, communities, families, and society.

In conclusion, play is essential for children's development and learning. It helps them to develop physically, cognitively, emotionally, and socially. It is a positive way for children to relieve stress and express themselves. Play also helps children to develop creativity, imagination, and problem-solving skills.

Chapter 8: How to Deal with Daily Challenges

Are you feeling overwhelmed by daily challenges? If so, our kids' guide to conquering daily challenges can help. It guides will teach you how to overcome any obstacle in your way, whether it's getting out of bed on time or finding the energy to make breakfast. We know this type of guidance is important for young adults who want to succeed and thrive. So, we're including a variety of topics, from health and fitness tips to tougher challenge ideas, so you can discovery what works best for your readers.

What are daily challenges and how can they be conquered.

Daily challenges can be everything from completing a task all day to overcoming a difficult obstacle. They can also have some bad consequences, such as anxiety or depression. If you are experiencing any of these conditions, daily challenges can be a great way to manage them and achieve success.

What are some common daily challenges and how can they be overcome

Some common daily challenges include completing tasks all day, solving an obstacle, or making new friends. You can overwhelm these tests by doing something that is challenging but safe and manageable, like reading a challenging book or playing a game. These activities will help you build confidence and skills so that you can tackle the next challenge head-on.

How to overcome daily challenges and achieve success

When conquering any everyday challenge, it takes time and practice. However, you can achieve your goals quickly and easily with the right tools and strategies. By following these tips, you will increase your chances of conquering your daily tasks and achieving success: Find someone who can help guide you through each step of the challenge; Practice regularly; Be persistent; Take positive focus on your progress; Stay organized; Have fun!

How to Conquer Daily Challenges.

A daily challenge can be anything from simple to overwhelming. To conquer them, you need to understand their different types and how to overcome them. There are six different types of daily challenges:

1. Puzzles

2. Goals

3. Timing

4. Money

5. Time Management

6. Physical Fitness

Tips for conquering daily challenges.

1. Find a way to amuse and engage your child while they are getting ready for the day.

2. Set simple goals that your child can complete without much difficulty.

3. Have fun activities for your child to do in between tasks, such as coloring or playing games.

1andowski how to overcome daily challenges.

One of the greatest significant belongings you can do to conquer daily challenges is to make them easier. Here are some tips to help:

-Find a routine that works for you and stick with it. It will help break down the day's challenge into manageable chunks.

-Talk to your doctor or therapist about any difficulties that are bothering you, and seek out advice on how to deal with them.

-Make sure you have everything you need before starting each task, including a planner, phone, water bottle, and snacks. It will help keep you motivated throughout the day.

-Be patient; many challenges can be overcome in time, but there will be times when progress is difficult to make. Don't give up!

Conquering daily challenges is difficult, but with the right tools and strategies, it can be done. By understanding the different types of daily challenges and conquering them one by one, you will be on your way to achieving success. Use the right tools to make everyday tasks easier and conquer daily challenges from scratch.

Chapter 9: Toolbox Therapy

In this chapter, you will absorb around tools that can be used to help improve your mental health, body and soul. You will also study how to find and use the resources that work best for you.

What is Toolbox Therapy.

Toolbox Therapy is a new way to help your mind, body, and soul. It is a system of self-care that uses tools and techniques to improve your emotional state. The benefits of Toolbox Therapy include:

1) increased emotional well-being

2) improved physical health

3) reduced stress levels and anxiety

4) improved communication and relationship skills

5) enhanced spiritual growth

What are the steps to using Toolbox Therapy

The first step in using Toolbox Therapy is to identify your needs. It will help you create a toolbox of techniques and tools that will best serve your individual needs. Next, you'll need to take the time to practice and use these tools according to your personal schedule and goals. Finally, keep track of your progress and update your toolbox as needed so you can continue making positive changes in your life.

How to use Toolbox Therapy

Toolbox Therapy begins with understanding yourself. After this, you'll need to find a support group or class that can provide you with additional tools, strategies, and support for improving your emotional state. You can also access resources online or in person from therapists who specialize in Toolbox Therapy. The bottom line is that by following the steps outlined in this chapter, you'll be able to experience increased emotional well-being, physical health, reduced stress levels and anxiety, improved communication and relationship skills, and enhanced spiritual growth – all while saving money on your trip!

How to Get started with Toolbox Therapy.

The first step in using Toolbox Therapy is to find a therapist who can provide you with the necessary training and guidance. Once you have a therapist, you will be able to start using the therapy session as a way to help yourself and your loved ones.

Learn More about Toolbox Therapy

To learn more about how to use Toolbox Therapy, begin by reading through our chapter on the subject. We will shelter all from how to get started with the therapy sessions to finding a therapist who can provide you with the necessary support.

Get Help from a Therapist

If you are feeling lost or uncomfortable during your first session of Toolbox Therapy, it may be helpful to seek out professional help soon. Many therapists are available 24/7, so don't hesitate to reach out if you need assistance starting or continuing therapy.

Make a plan to use Toolbox Therapy according to your needs and goals. Once you have a plan, stick to it and start using the therapy as soon as possible.

Find a therapist who is familiar with Toolbox Therapy. A therapist who is familiar with Toolbox Therapy can help you better understand and use the therapy.

Use the resources obtainable to you to study additional about Toolbox Therapy. There are many books, articles, websites, and other resources available to help you learn more about Toolbox Therapy.

Be patient and enjoy the benefits of Toolbox Therapy. For most people, using Toolbox Therapy will result in long-lasting effects. Be patient and enjoy the many benefits that come with using this type of therapy!

Toolbox Therapy is a helpful and effective way to improve mental health. By starting with one session, you can see the biggest benefits immediately. Additionally, it's important to find a therapist who is familiar with the therapy and use the resources available to you to learn more about it. Be patient and enjoy the benefits of Toolbox Therapy!

Chapter 10: 150 Fun Activities

REVERSE WORDS

You should encourage your kid to have fun with words by giving them a fresh twist since her language abilities are blossoming. Try saying words and sentences backward!

Materials and Tools:

Context of a Meal

Instructions with necessary skills:

You may help your youngster learn the game while conversing in everyday language by playing it at meals.

Saying basic phrases backward might be a good start; try "More milk, please" and "Thank you."

Show her how to play many times to ensure she gets it.

As your kid improves, you may go on to more complex phrases.

Alternately, you may have a backward hour in which you spoke and acted reversely. Alternative: play out a reverse scene from a book you both love!

If your youngster is having trouble following the game, try using simpler phrases with only two words or waiting a few days before trying again.

QUITE USEFUL

Make your kid use their creativity to see what they can make from a handprint!

Materials and Tools:

Pieces of paper Felt-tip pens

Instructions with necessary skills:

Create many handprints on paper using your kid's hand.

Allow her to express her creativity by giving her a chance to paint her hands in whatever way she sees fit, whether it is a turkey, rooster, flower garden, face with huge hair, sunrise, humorous creature, porcupine, etc.

Look at all the cool stuff she can build with her hand print!

Try sketching your child's feet and seeing what they come up with.

Warning: Only use child-safe, non-toxic pens.

TUB FOR WASHING CARS

The Car-Wash Bath is so fun and educational that even youngsters who normally dread baths can't wait to take one.

Materials and Tools:

Essentials for a relaxing soak in the tub, including the tub itself, bubble bath, eyewear, sponges, washcloths, shampoo, soap, spray bottles, squirt bottles, towels, and lotion

Instructions with necessary skills:

Prepare a hot bath by filling the tub.

As the water in the bathtub fills, pour in some bubble bath.

Put your kid in the bath and give him some goggles to protect his eyes.

Use sponges and washcloths to sponge him down.

Using shampoo and soap, give him a full body scrub.

Use squirt guns to wipe the grime off him as you would a vehicle.

Towel him down.

To wax him, use lotion. Zero stains!

Swap out the bathtub for the shower and carry out the same steps. There's a vehicle wash where your kid can go, too!

Warning: Keep soap away from your kid's eyes. Additionally, check that the

The water shouldn't be too hot, and you should keep an eye on him to make sure he doesn't slide. Never assume that your kid is safe when they are in the tub.

INTEND TO DYE MY HANDS A DIFFERENT COLOR?

Create a coloring book of your kid's bodily parts to help her learn about them. First, focus on her hand, then go up her arm to her elbows and face, and then down to her tummy, knees, and feet.

Materials and Tools:

Copier Crayons or felt-tip pens

Instructions with necessary skills:

Try this: put your kid's hand on the photocopier's glass.

Put the copier cover over her hand.

Don't want her eyes to become too strained by the copy machine's strong light, so have her shut them.

Simply by pressing the button, copies will be made.

Feel free to take the duplicate home with you. Have her trace the hand using a black felt-tip pen if the copy quality isn't great, then have her color it in with felt-tip pens or crayons.

Give her permission to accessorize whatever she sees fit by adding rings, fingernails, manicure paint, bracelets, etc.

Alternative: photocopy many body pieces and have your kid assemble them when you get home. If she wants to find out what type of wacky character she becomes, she may fill in the drawings and find out!

Warning: Have your kiddo keep her eyes closed throughout the copying process. Do the same for your safety.

STICK TO THE MARKS

Try this twist on the classic treasure hunt to keep your kid interested in finding the clues. The road can take you wherever you want it to.

Materials and Tools:

Large play space a dozen or more bright stickers a cracker or other treat

Instructions with necessary skills:

Get yourself a bunch of bright stickers.

Make your kid a path to follow throughout the home and yard.

Stickers should be placed every few feet along the path so that hikers may easily see them.

Throw in a reward at the finish line.

Send your kid in, telling him to seek for a sticker trail that will bring him to a reward.

When he finds it, tell him how lucky he is.

You may change things up by increasing the distance between the stickers for each new game. Have your little one draws up a sticker trail for you, too! It's all up to him to plot out the path and decide on the reward.

Caution: Keep your kid away from sharp items and high places.

RACE CAR

A child's mind and body may be opened to limitless possibilities with only a box.

Materials and Tools:

You'll need a big box (about half your kid's size), scissors or an X-acto knife, duct tape, felt-tip pens, crayons, paint, stickers, decals, fringe, and a book on automobiles and trucks.

Instructions with necessary skills:

Together, you may learn a lot about automobiles and trucks by reading and analyzing a picture book.

To make a smaller box, remove the top and bottom but leave the sides intact.

Duct tape may be used to strengthen corners and smooth off sharp edges.

Use paint, stickers, and other embellishments to transform the exterior of the box into a vehicle your kid will love.

Give your kid a spin in the automobile around the home or yard after it's done.

Use rope to mark off lanes and place roadblocks at strategic points for some extra amusement.

Alternative: instead of an automobile, your youngster may take off in a homemade aircraft or boat.

Caution: If your youngster is around, they should not use scissors or an X-acto knife.

SPEECH RECORDING

Tape records your youngster talking and play it back for him or her; children like hearing their voices. Listen to all the various voices she can create!

Materials and Tools:

Equipment: Cassette player, microphone, and a blank cassette

Instructions with necessary skills:

To use the cassette recorder, a blank tape must first be inserted.

Pick a fun question, like "What did you do at preschool?" for your kid to answer. Is there anything specific you'd want on your special day? substitute "What did you think of (insert name of popular TV program here)?"

Play the tape, go near to her lips with the microphone, and record her thoughts on the matter.

Here, let's listen to her voice on the recording.

Choose another subject and have her recite it using a voice that is extremely low, very high, that of a cartoon character, and so on.

Get your youngster to use different voices for each segment, then play the recording backwards to hear how they progressed.

Try taping your loved ones and having your kid identify them to switch things up.

If the tape player requires an electrical outlet, instruct your youngster to stay away from the power cable. Check that she doesn't accidentally hit any buttons on the recorder.

DO SOME WRITING

Inspire your youngster to be creative by having her write and illustrate her book, exactly like the ones she'll find at the library.

Materials and Tools:

Craft supplies Felt-tip pens Paper, glue, tape, scissors, and stapler Children's magazines or low-cost picture books

Instructions with necessary skills:

Take eight to ten photographs from a children's magazine or a picture book and cut them out.

Spread out the artwork on the floor so everyone can have a look.

Print off the photos (one per page) and glue them onto regular paper, allowing space at the bottom for some text.

Put all the photographs in a stack and have your youngster choose one at a time until he or she has picked them all.

Then, cover the pile with a blank piece of paper and bind the papers together with a stapler.

Have your youngster start a tale based on the first photo by describing what they see.

Observe what she says and jot it down underneath the image.

When you get to the next image in the tale, have her turn the page and look at it while you continue to narrate and take notes below.

Go on until you get to the last page of the book.

Give her the top sheet and tell her to come up with a title.

Take turns reading the story.

A variant: have your kid narrate a story while you take notes. Then, ask her to illustrate the story. When the book is done, you should tell the story again.

Caution: Be cautious with the stapler and scissors while you work. You might also consider recording her so you can transcribe it afterwards.

JOIN FORCES?

Engage your kid's creativity by asking her to invent a matching game once you've taught her how to pair like objects.

Materials and Tools:

Things that are often found in pairs, such as shoes and socks, pens and paper, spoons and plates, washcloths and toothbrushes, combs and ribbons, ketchup and mustard, etc.

Instructions with necessary skills:

Collect a number of sets of complementary but distinct objects.

Sort the objects into two piles, one containing pairs.

Set the first stack in front of your kid on the floor or a table.

Show your kid an item from the other stack that matches one they have.

Ask her to choose the appropriate thing.

Make room by putting the paired items aside and picking something else.

Keep going until everything has a matching pair.

You should talk about the similarities and differences between the things.

Allow your youngster to take a turn in gathering pairs for you to sort.

Put everything on the floor or table and let your kid choose the pairs they like most.

Take care, you need to make sure they're safe to handle.

TAKE A GUESS AT THE FINAL STAGE

Encourage your kid to try to guess what happens next in a tale. The expertise will serve him well in many sorts of mental endeavors, particularly in the realm of problem solving.

Materials and Tools:

A children's book with a cliffhanger conclusion

Instructions with necessary skills:

Find a contented spot to curl up with the book.

Take turns reading aloud to your youngster, stopping just short of the last page.

Inquire as to his forecast.

I would advise him to consider a number of alternatives for the story's conclusion.

In order to learn how the narrative concludes, please read the remainder of the book.

Compare and contrast the real conclusion with the other versions he came up with.

Carry this process further with other books.

Optional change: see the film's prologue. Proceed as described above, but this time pause halfway through to talk about potential conclusions.

Warning: it's best to choose stories where the protagonist triumphs over adversity and the conclusion leaves the reader feeling fulfilled. If you don't help, your kid could become upset.

TAKE A GUESS?

Your youngster will quickly figure out what's on your mind if you give them enough hints. Ignore her and let her test you instead!

Materials and Tools:

Space containing a variety of fascinating objects

Instructions with necessary skills:

Choose something in the room that will grab people's attention and hold it, like a figurine.

Explain to your kid that you're trying to think of anything and offer her a hint, such the object's color, size, or form.

Get her to attempt and identify the object.

Just offer your kid another hint and let her try again if she gets it wrong.

Keep going until she gets the right answer.

The next time your kid wants to help you find anything, give them a turn picking out an item and giving you hints.

This is an amusing game to show while waiting in line or on the road.

Warning: Keep the item where everyone can see it. In addition, avoid picking anything that might harm your kid.

VARIOUS NOISES

Get your kid to practice telling the difference between similar-sounding words. Eventually, he'll become an excellent listener if he engages in this activity.

Materials and Tools:

Different pairings of objects from many categories, including: a can opener and a blender, a doorbell and a telephone, a piano and a guitar, a puppy and a cat, a bouncing ball and a stacking block, a cassette recorder and a tape, and so on.

Instructions with necessary skills:

Gather a number of pairs of similar objects and record the noises they make.

Get a table and put the smaller things on it.

Take the recording into your child's room and ask him or her to listen for the source of the sound. In order to locate the piano or the pets, he may have to do some exploring of the home. If he needs additional time, pause the recording and let him repeat the noises.

Your youngster will learn more about comparison and contrast by sorting the objects into pairs once he or she has identified each sound.

You may switch things up by not putting anything on the table and instead playing the tape and having your kid guess what's being shown. You might also have him point out an object that creates a certain sound, and then play only that sound while he picks out a similar-sounding item.

Warning: keep the tape recorder's volume down and stay away from anything spooky.

noises.

FEEDBACK, ME DOLL

What kid wouldn't like making a paper version of themselves to play with? He'll undoubtedly want to expand his doll collection to include others in the family.

Materials and Tools:

Glue Scissors Photograph of your kid Photographs of family members (optional) Paper doll package

Instructions with necessary skills:

Depending on your kid's age, pick up a paper dolls bundle.

Make a silhouette of your kid's head from a snapshot.

Attach this piece to the top of the doll's head using glue.

Your youngster may also enjoy making paper dolls of other family members.

Those paper dolls are perfect for your kid to play with.

Another option is to have your youngster act out a narrative about their family using the paper dolls as puppets.

Use caution while working with sharp objects and adhesives around a youngster.

DO SOME SNEAKING AROUND

Have you tried peeping a tiny bit at the mystery object to see if your kid can guess what it is? This is because her ability to deduce becomes more refined the more she observes.

Materials and Tools:

Several visually engaging big objects, such as a plush animal, piece of clothing, picture book, toy vehicle, baby doll, jigsaw, etc. Large paper bag to transport the objects Cloth, towel, or small blanket

Instructions with necessary skills:

Gather your belongings and arrange them in a paper bag.

Use the cloth to reach inside the sack and pull out a single object while keeping it covered.

Place the swaddled object in the middle of you and your kid.

Show just a tiny section of the object at a time.

Ask your kid to attempt to guess what it is.

Do not stop revealing details until she properly identifies them.

You must repeat the procedure to the rest of the bag's contents.

An alternative is to show your youngster the goods before placing them in the bag. Making it such that you can only reference images of the goods added an extra level of difficulty.

Carefully choose products that your toddler can safely handle.

HARD PARTS OF ANIMALS

Put your kid to work finding the corresponding animal heads and tails. Or, you could just let her make up her wild animals.

Materials and Tools:

Magazine or cheap book animal pictures Scissors Glue or paste Sheets of construction paper Surface to work on

Instructions with necessary skills:

Separate images of various animals and cut them out.

Split the images in two, one for the head and one for the body.

Set the severed heads in front of your kid on the ground or a table.

Choose a tail piece and give it to her so she can put it together with the right head.

Give her a piece of construction paper and have her glue each finished animal onto it.

All the animals need to be reunited, so keep doing this until you've finished.

Alternatively, your kid may play around with the idea of matching heads and tails on purpose to make new, amusing creatures.

Once you're done cutting apart the photos, put the scissors away and keep an eye out for your kid putting glue in her mouth.

RHYTHMIC RHYME

Teach your kid to keep time and expand their vocabulary all at once! It takes approximately practice to master, but the game makes conversation a blast.

Materials and Tools:

Music (optional)

Instructions with necessary skills:

Consider a simple word to rhyme with, such as "goat."

Start with modest clapping and try to keep the beat with your youngster.

Clap your hands as you yell the word.

While you keep clapping, have your kid utter a word that rhymes with it.

Keep clapping in time as he comes up with fresh rhymes. As an alternative, you may take it in turns generating rhymes until you're stumped.

Simply choose a new term and start again.

A variant: sing or recite the rhymes to the accompaniment of music.

Caution: Explicit language ahead.

SCARF DANCE

A child's imagination may flourish and her motor skills can be honed with as little as a handful of scarves. Play some tunes and see the scarves fly!

Materials and Tools:

Two scarves, each at least as long as your kid is tall 2 wooden utensils of some kind Extensive Room player cassette loaded with music

Instructions with necessary skills:

To make a scarf chopstick, just tie one end of each scarf to a chopstick.

PLAY SOME TUNES

Let your kid wave the scarves about while holding a stick in each hand.

If she wants the scarves to move more in time with the music, have her dance about while waving them.

You should ask her to put together some basic choreography for a scarf dance to the tunes.

Swap places and dance with her while she uses the scarf stick, you're not using. Try tying the scarves in a knot every so often and seeing what happens!

Take care to clear the passage of any obstructions. Keep the scarf from being tied around your kid's neck; she may easily trip over it.

DO THE JUMP, SKIPPY, AND HOP

If your kid doesn't pay attention to a few basic directions, he could skip when he should have hopped or leaped.

Materials and Tools:

Extensive Room

Instructions with necessary skills:

Make sure your youngster has enough of space to do the exercises by standing in a broad, clutter-free location.

Ask him to skip, hop, or leap based on your order.

Give him a new directive, and he'll move on to that.

Keep shouting orders, but increase your pace until he falls with laughter.

Play again, this time with directions to dance, twirl, jump, etc.

Take a trip about your neighborhood while naming various walking styles as you go (slow, quick, backwards, sideways, tiny, large, skipping, hopping, jumping, etc.). Another option is to model different walking styles for your kid to imitate.

Caution: If your kid is becoming upset or confused, slow down the instructions or put the game away.

ZOOMING AROUND

Your little one may enjoy themselves by mimicking the animal's gait. Assist him in making imaginary motions with his limbs, head, and torso.

Materials and Tools:

Picture books featuring large creatures with characteristic gaits, such as ducks, crabs, frogs, kangaroos, elephants, inchworms, chickens, rabbits, seals, snakes, and caterpillars, etc.

Instructions with necessary skills:

Browse a library full of animal image books.

Encourage your youngster to walk like the animals in the stories you're reading to him while you read.

You may assist him by explaining the actions and providing visuals if required. Let him see how a duck waddles, a crab travels laterally, a kangaroo jumps, an elephant lumbers, an inchworm inches, a chicken lunges, a rabbit hops, a seal slides, a snake slithers, and a caterpillar executes a caterpillar walk.

The rules may change such that players take turns emulating an animal's gait and fooling their opponent into guessing their species.

Take care to cleanse the area of any potential hazards.

IT'S A TIP OF THE TAP

Enjoy some lighthearted time with your fingers by playing the game of Tippy Tap. Tell your kid to make his fingers perform the talking, walking, and tapping!

Materials and Tools:

Ten tiny thimbles or pen tops a resolutely solid surface

Instructions with necessary skills:

Thimbles or pen caps may protect your child's fingers. Thimbles and pen caps may not fit properly without first covering his fingers with little Band-Aids.

Give your kid a table or other hard surface and teach them to tap out a beat.

Put on some tunes and have him tap along with the beat.

Have him move his fingers over different surfaces in the room and take note of the noises he creates.

Swap thimbles and tap out a song on various parts of your body. Blindfold him and ask him to identify the body area you're tapping.

Be careful that your youngster doesn't put the tapers of his pens in his mouth, and avoid using pen caps with pointy edges. Avoid having your kid tap on glass or anything else that might shatter.

TAPPER SHOES

Children enjoy earshot their voices and will find this game equally amusing when it comes to hearing their footsteps. Toe Tappers, with their flashing lights, will help your baby be heard.

Materials and Tools:

Flat metal washers the size of your child's foot, or a pair of old, beat-up sneakers Surface adhesive superglue

Instructions with necessary skills:

Try to track down a pair of your kid's old, worn-out shoes that you were planning on throwing away, or pick up a new pair from a secondhand store.

Add two flat metal washers to the shoe's toe and two to the heel using superglue. Get it dry.

Put the shoes on your kid and take her for a stroll on the concrete.

Play some music and teach her to tap to the beat.

Alternately: splurge on a pair of gently-used tap shoes so she may get the whole authentic experience.

Warning: If the shoes don't fit completely, your youngster should avoid walking on slick areas and use additional caution while walking. Always use caution while working with superglue.

GRAPHIC INFORMATICS

Assist your kid in discovering the world around him by touching things. Advise him to try visualizing how he is feeling.

Materials and Tools:

Many little, varied textures that your kid can fit in his or her hand, such as a plush animal, washcloth, cup, cracker, ball, etc. Wearing a paper bag over your eyes (optional)

Instructions with necessary skills:

Grab a paper bag and fill it with various objects with varying textures and/or shapes.

Place yourself on the floor opposite your kid.

Wrap a blindfold across his eyes or tell him to shut them.

Take something out of the bag and give it to your kid.

Get him to take a good, hard feel of the object and try to identify it.

If his guesses are off, give him some pointers.

You may modify the preceding instructions by showing your youngster the objects before blindfolding him.

If your kid hates wearing blindfolds, you may always just tell him to shut his eyes and not peek. Verify if it is safe to handle the products.

SPOT THE VARIED CUBES OF COLOR

Even when she's getting clean, your kid might be teaching herself valuable new abilities.

Materials and Tools:

Prepare a hot tub, food coloring, and an ice cube tray.

Instructions with necessary skills:

Use food coloring to make ice cubes of various hues. Make sure the cubes are frozen before you go in the tub.

Prepare a hot tub for soaking.

Submerge your youngster in the water.

Allow your youngster to try to catch the colored ice cubes as you drop them one by one into the water. She has to act fast, since the slick cubes will start to melt in the hot water.

Ice should be added gradually until the glass is completely full.

Periodically filling the tub with hot water may be required.

You may also test how long it takes for a tiny toy to sink by placing it on top of an ice cube. Alternatively, you might freeze a tiny toy within an ice cube for a humorous twist.

Save an eye on your kid while they're in the tub, and keep the water at a comfortable temperature.

WHERE IS IT ABSENT?
Choosing fun objects makes it more enjoyable for your kid to guess what's missing.

Materials and Tools:

Set of four to six objects, including but not limited to a toy, food, book, article of clothing, and so on. a sheet, a blanket, a towel

Instructions with necessary skills:

Put them on the ground or a table in front of your kid.

Once he's finished looking at them, call them out one by one and say what they are.

Use a blanket or towel to conceal the things.

Look at the list and ensure you know what everything is called.

Don't let your kid watch you taking away an item.

Take away the blanket and list what is left.

Try asking your kid, "What's missing?"

To get rid of another item, simply go back through the steps 4–7 again.

Restart the game with a fresh set of materials.

To increase the difficulty, you may increase the number of objects you're allowed to utilize or the options you're given.

ones that are more closely connected, or skip the evaluation process altogether. You may make the game easier by either reducing the number of things or reviewing them several times.

Take care, you need to make sure they're safe to touch.

THIRD PARTY GARMENTS?
This game is great for helping your toddler discover the differences between males and females.

Materials and Tools:

People-filled magazines Scissors A flat surface

Instructions with necessary skills:

People of all sexes, ages, and sizes may be found in magazines and made into cutouts.

Then, use scissors to create silhouettes of men's, women's, children's, and infants' garments.

Arrange the portraits of individuals in front of your kid on the ground or a table.

Do not put any distance between you and the garment photographs.

Take the first garment photo and show it to your kid.

Ask her to pair it with the appropriate male, female, male, or female.

Keep going until all the garments have been assigned to their respective wearers.

Change things up by enlisting your kid's assistance in determining which clothes belong to whom in the family laundry pile.

Caution: Always supervise your youngster while they are around scissors.

SOFT AND INVITING SEATING

Instructions with necessary skills:

Choose a book with a thrilling tale that can be read to a child.

Grab a comfy chair and start reading a bedtime tale to your little one.

Alter the text as you go so that the images no longer make sense. When he wears the men, change the color of Curious George's hat from yellow to red.

Take a breather after adjusting to see how your kid responds. It should be obvious to him that you've interpreted the situation differently.

Even if he doesn't say anything, you should definitely question him whether what you read is accurate.

Don't rush him into accepting the shift; let him mull it through.

If at all feasible, you should have him make the adjustment.

Do something else with the plot now, and turn the page.

Keep on till the tale is through.

Try a new spin on this game by having your youngster retell the tale to you while substituting his words for the ones in the original text.

Warning: Don't choose a book that will give you nightmares.

READING MATERIAL

Assist your kid in writing a story in which he plays the main character.

Materials and Tools:

Pieces of white paper Picture periodicals Baby pictures and family portraits Works of art created by your kid Scissors Tools: Staple Gun and Glue Pen

Instructions with necessary skills:

Collect the photographs that mean the most to your kid, whether they be his artwork, pictures from magazines he enjoys, pictures of family members, etc.

Put each thing on a separate piece of white paper and glue it down.

Instruct him to explain the importance of each image, and record his explanations at the page's end.

Bind the papers together with staples, then add a cover sheet that says, "All About Me!"

After you've completed the book, you may read it aloud.

Alternate version: At any time, your kid may insert new pages into the book. Maybe he should break it up into chapters.

Warning: make sure you have backup copies of any irreplaceable family pictures. Be careful with scissors around your child.

ANIMAKER

Have your youngster build her kind of creatures and watch what weird things she comes up with!

Materials and Tools:

Animal illustrations from periodicals and cheap picture books Scissors Tabletop Paper Adhesive Tape

Instructions with necessary skills:

Animal photographs were cut out of magazines.

Separate the images of the animals into their respective sections, such as a head, a body, legs, a tail, and so on.

Put the body pieces in a pile and let your kiddo mix them up.

Then, have her choose different organs so she can assemble new creatures.

Assist her with placing the various bodily parts on a piece of paper in whichever fashion she sees fit by using glue or tape.

Do it again and again until all or almost all of the components have been utilized.

A kid may need your assistance in giving their animal creations proper names.

Try this alternative: have your kid sketch completely made-up creatures.

A word of caution while working with scissors and glue: keep them away from your kid.

CREATE A BUBBLE BATH

In the process of playing and getting clean, you may introduce your kid to some of water's fascinating characteristics.

Materials and Tools:

Bubble solution for the bathroom

Instructions with necessary skills:

Put your kid in a tub full of hot water.

To add some fun to your bath, crack up a bottle of bubble solution and go blowing! Try to get your kid to burst the bubbles before they hit the water.

Fill the tub with bubble solution, give your kid a straw, and see whether he can blow bubbles in the water.

Alternative: Go outdoors and attempt to capture bubbles you blow.

You should use caution while removing your kid from the tub since the bubble solution will make the surface slippery. Make sure he doesn't accidentally breathe in any bubble water either.

ALTER A NARRATIVE

Expectation for the following chapter is a fun activity for kids. Have some fun and see whether your youngster notices when you alter the tale from what he is expecting.

Materials and Tools:

a story-driven picture book like "Where the Wild Things Are," "Curious George," "Clifford the Big Red Dog," or "Arthur."

WHAT OCCURED?

The best time to teach a youngster to think ahead and find solutions to issues is before they arise. Make it interesting for her to find answers.

Materials and Tools:

Captivating narrative in the form of a picture book.

Instructions with necessary skills:

Choose a picture book in which your kid can guess what will happen next.

Put on some comfy chairs and start reading the narrative together.

Keep your kid involved by asking her what she thinks will happen next and then turning the page to see if she was right.

Now let's turn the page and find out whether she was correct.

Keep reading till the last page.

Another option is to use magazine photographs as inspiration for tales rather than picture books. Ask her, "What happened?" to get the conversation rolling.

Choosing books carefully is important so as not to scare your kid, especially with stories about death.

PRIDE PROCESSION IN COLOR

You may aid your child's color recognition by taking her on a "Color Walk," during which you and she will observe the many hues seen in your immediate environment.

Materials and Tools:

Vibrantly colored room, yard, or park

Instructions with necessary skills:

You should take your kid out for a stroll.

Ask her to choose a color while you go along.

Get her to look for as many examples of that hue as she can find.

Have her choose a new color to search for once she discovers 10 objects.

You may up the difficulty by choosing a different color for each person before you set out on your stroll. In this game, the first player to locate 10 objects of her chosen color gets to pick the following two colors.

Be careful not to hurt yourself by stumbling over any obstacles on your quest to find every color!

SPOKEN TWICE

Here's a fun approach to help your kid pick up more words: engage in a lot of Double Talk with them.

Materials and Tools:

Your child's day at preschool, her favorite book or TV program, her new toy, and so on are all great conversation starters.

Instructions with necessary skills:

Pick an issue to talk about with your kid.

Ask her to start a tale by reciting it to you word by word.

Get her to pause when she finishes speaking so you may repeat what she says word for word.

Keep on with the tale till she's finished.

Switch places: you narrate the narrative, and she retells it as accurately as she can.

To change things up, have her utter a few lines and see how quickly you can repeat them. The tables should be turned. You may have her write more complex sentences as she improves. Make the game harder by adding additional words.

Caution: If your youngster isn't enjoying the copying portion, either stop the game and try again in a few days or explain what you're doing again.

DOES-A-DO?

This is a great way to work on mental and physical skills simultaneously!

Materials and Tools:

Tools, such a rope, ball, blanket, block, spoon, hat, towel, and so on, and a clean, empty space to use them in

Instructions with necessary skills:

Acquire a number of functional objects.

Home them on the ground in front of you and the kid.

Pick one thing (a ball, for instance) and pose the question, "What does a ball do?" to your kid.

Get him to explain the item's function, and then prod him to demonstrate it.

Try to elicit from him a list of other uses for the item. A ball, for instance, may be bounced, caught, tossed, sat on, rolled, flattened, kicked, carried, and so on.

Move on to the next item and do it again.

You may switch things up by letting your kid choose out a few items and then explaining their use. Also, be sure to provide evidence.

Warning: make sure anything you're working with is secure and not harmful to touch.

TAG WITH FLASHLIGHT

A game that is both entertaining to play in the dark and instructive for developing spatial awareness is provided.

Materials and Tools:

Two torches, one dimly lit room

Instructions with necessary skills:

Donate one flashlight to your kid and retain the other for yourself.

Enter a room and switch off the lights.

Turn on the flashlight and have your kid chase you around the room with it, 4. When he finally finds you, you're out of luck. It's your time to shine a light on your kid now.

Flip the script and see whether your kid can use his flashlight to discover something you hid in the dark. It wouldn't hurt to give him a hint.

Avoid giving your kid any reason to be scared of the dark by removing any potential hazards from the play space.

JUST HANG ON TO THE LINE

Put your kid on a rope and let her explore some creepy caves!

Materials and Tools:

length of yarn, rope, or other similar material

Instructions with necessary skills:

Get a really long piece of yarn, thread, or rope.

Start at one end of the room or yard and work your way to the other, laying the rope on the ground or floor as you go.

To get the rope around the various obstructions, you'll need to twist it in various directions.

Let your kid get on the rope and walk it all the way to the finish line.

Warn that if she loses her balance, she will have to start again.

Have your kid walk the rope in reverse once she finishes the course for a little variety.

If you're using a rope to help your kid up, watch carefully so that it doesn't cross anything that may damage them if they fall.

GRADUATION CAPS OFF

Just by adding a hat, one's whole demeanor may be altered. Take a look at your kid's reaction when you put a cap on his head.

Materials and Tools:

baseball caps, feathered hats, scarves, cowboy hats, chef hats, fireman helmets, Mickey Mouse hats, and other headwear from a thrift store or costume shop

Instructions with necessary skills:

Get together a collection of headwear.

You can help your kid realize who he is by standing in front of a mirror.

Coat his head with the first one.

Provide him with a mirror and let him ogle his reflection.

Then have him act like someone who would normally wear that hat.

If you want to play along, choose a hat and pretend to be that person.

Use the hats to put on a play.

Swap up your headwear for some unique looks and play out some different roles.

Alternately, you might supplement the caps with additional costume accessories. The joy is in combining different kinds.

Take care to ensure the garments are free of any hazards, such as pins or sharp edges.

I AM CAPABLE OF IT!

Raise your child's self-awareness by pointing out her many strengths. This is an excellent strategy for bolstering her sense of personal worth and confidence.

Materials and Tools:

Pictures of youngsters being active in magazines or books for children

Instructions with necessary skills:

Peruse publications or picture books that feature children engaged in activities together.

See whether your kid can replicate the moves by asking her.

Get her to break down the steps she uses to do them.

If she wants to show off, let her!

Ask her why she thinks she can't accomplish anything if she claims she can't.

Talk to her about the limits placed on your actions. Specify your reasoning for accepting or rejecting the proposal.

Optional twist: Prompt your kid to attempt a task she hasn't mastered yet but believes she can, like pouring milk, tying her shoes, brushing her teeth, getting dressed, etc. Do everything you can to assist her.

Be careful to choose several images depicting things your kid is already competent at, so she doesn't feel discouraged. Do not coerce her into doing things she is not

not prepared to take on at this time

ILLUSTRATOR

Rather of using stock illustrations, encourage your youngster to create his .

Materials and Tools:

White paper, colored pencils, or felt-tip pens, a stapler, and a table

Instructions with necessary skills:

Set up a table with some paper and crayons or felt-tip pencils.

Partially make up a narrative and tell it to your youngster.

Ask him to sketch a picture of what's going on when you get to a good halting location.

Continue the tale and make him draw further pictures when he completes the first one.

Staple his work together when you're done reading and the kid is done sketching.

Step by step, you should look through his photographs and jot down the story's key details next to the images that best represent it.

Pick up a picture book and retell the tale to your kid for a change of pace. Have your youngster sketch a picture to go along with what you read on each page. Staple his drawings together after you're done with the tale. The two of you should read the children's book aloud and then contrast his drawings with those in the book.

Take cautious while using a stapler near a youngster.

COME ON, MUMMY UP

Make your kid seem like a monster by wrapping her in toilet paper.

Materials and Tools:

a full-length mirror and a roll of crepe paper or colorful toilet paper

Instructions with necessary skills:

Consider picking up a roll of crepe paper, a roll of toilet paper in pastel tones, or a roll of printed toilet paper.

Tell your kid to stop slouching and stand up straight.

Use the paper to wrap her up from head to toe, but avoid covering her face. She has to be wrapped up from head to toe.

If a piece of paper comes free, simply tuck it in and keep going.

When you're done, have your kid gaze in the mirror. Remember to snap a photo!

Make her move her limbs slowly and rigidly like a mummy!

Change it up: have your kid use toilet paper to wrap you up!

Avoid scaring your kid or preventing her from breathing by not covering her eyes, nose, or mouth.

EXTREMELY POWERFUL MEGAPHONE

A Mighty Megaphone might be the perfect tool to encourage your youngster to expand his or her vocabulary.

Materials and Tools:

Materials and Tools: a paper towel tube, stickers, contact paper, or felt-tip pens

Instructions with necessary skills:

Get yourself a used paper towel roll.

Use stickers, contact paper, or felt-tip pencils to adorn the tube.

Talk to your youngster normally, then demonstrate using the Mighty Megaphone to amplify your voice.

Use the megaphone to hear his tales!

Make two megaphones and have fun having a two-way dialogue with your kid.

To avoid injury, instruct your youngster to avoid jogging while holding the megaphone to his lips.

HOME OF MY OWN

Your child's bedroom is important to her growing sense of self. Assist her in recognizing the unique qualities of her bedroom and, by extension, herself.

Materials and Tools:

Table Large sheet of paper with felt-tip pens

Instructions with necessary skills:

Spread out a big piece of paper on the table.

Draw a bedroom floor plan, including the entrance, windows, closet, and bed, and explain their functions to your kid.

Just ask her what else she has in her room.

To help her remember what she has in her room, she draws and names each object as she goes through her inventory.

Give her hints if she seems to have forgotten anything.

Visit her room afterward to find out how much she retained.

To switch things up, challenge your kid to sketch her bedroom without any parental input. Also, get her talking about the items she keeps in her room and why she values them.

Caution: Only use felt-tip pens that aren't poisonous.

CONSTRUCT A RESIDENCE

Construct a house with your kiddo. Just get a big cardboard box, some art supplies, and your creative juices will flow!

Materials and Tools:

Appliance box, scissors, X-acto knife, duct tape, poster paints, decals, stickers, fringe, self-adhesive felt squares, and other embellishments

Instructions with necessary skills:

Start by contacting a nearby appliance retailer for a large box, or searching through your family's storage areas for one left over from the purchase of a new refrigerator, washing machine, or wide-screen television.

Cut a horizontal slit along the top, down one side, and down the bottom the same distance as the top to create a door in one side of the box. Let a crease on the side that wasn't cut to make the door swing freely.

Remove glass from walls in the same way. You may either leave one side uncut to enable your youngster to open and shut the window, or cut all four sides to make it permanent.

Fill up gaps, buff off sharp corners, then reinforce the underside with duct tape.

Instruct your youngster in the use of felt-tip pens, stickers, decals, and other home embellishments.

Let her decorate the home with anything she likes, including little chairs, cushions, toys, and more.

Permit her to act out the role of housewife.

Help your kid construct a house, a store, a fire station, or anything else they may imagine. She can create a whole metropolis!

Use extreme caution while using an X-acto knife near a youngster. Use paints and felt-tip pens that are suitable for use around children.

ACT LIKE ME AND YOU'LL GET WHAT YOU WANT

Does your kid try to mimic your voice? Have her try to imitate your made-up voices for different characters.

Materials and Tools:

Images of people, babies, animals, cartoons, TV characters, and other fictional personalities.

Instructions with necessary skills:

A fun activity is to compile a photo album of fictional people.

Give your kid a look at the first photo.

Use a silly and imaginative voice to imitate the protagonist.

Tell your kid to attempt to mimic your voice and character's dialogue.

Iterate this process for the other roles, varying your voice for each one.

Have your youngster use their imagination and give the characters their voices for some more fun.

Be careful not to yell and damage each other's hearing!

EGG NOG PAINT

Did you really believe that? Let your kid experience the joy of playing with pudding instead.

Materials and Tools:

Protective clothing Pudding (either from a box or in a pre-packaged container) Spoons Food coloring (optional)

Instructions with necessary skills:

Put on a smock to shield your kid's clothing from the mess.

Combine the pudding ingredients, or empty the ready-to-eat pudding into a serving dish.

For further excitement, dye some vanilla pudding.

You may use a clean tabletop, or you can put down some shiny paper.

Spread the pudding out on the paper or the table.

Give your kid some pudding and encourage him or her to be creative with it.

The leftovers are for him to enjoy after he's done!

Alternative: replace the pudding with shaving cream or whipped cream for a new experience.

Warn your youngster not to put the shaving cream on his face or in his mouth.

BODY ON WHEELS

Your kid will love getting a massage while growing in self-awareness and sensitivity to touch.

Materials and Tools:

Scratch-free blanket carpeted floor and sanitary rolling pin

Instructions with necessary skills:

To protect a rolling pin from damage, wrap it in a washcloth and tape the ends together.

Cover the carpet with a blanket.

Encourage your kid to shut her eyes and rest on her stomach on the blanket.

While singing a tune, gently roll the rolling pin over her body. Don't forget to squish all of her limbs and organs.

As you work your way down one side, flip her over and do the other.

When you're done with both sides, let your kid roll the pin over you for more fun!

Make sure the massage doesn't become too painful by rolling the pin too quickly. Warn her to take care with the rolling pin should she unintentionally strike you with it.

COOK UP SOMETHING OUTRAGEOUS

You must spend as greatly time as possible in the kitchen with your kid since it's a countless way to impart him or her valuable life skills.

Materials and Tools:

Cake pans (either round, square, or shaped like your favorite cartoon character), yellow or white cake mix, mixing bowls, measuring spoons, food coloring, colorful sprinkles, a can of frosting, decorating tubes, and any other edible embellishments you'd like, and an oven.

Instructions with necessary skills:

Get a cake mix, either white or yellow.

Instruct your kiddo to follow the package's instructions as they measure, pour, stir, and combine.

Allow your youngster to add a few drops of food coloring of his choosing to the prepared batter.

Give him free reign to create a pattern with the color, or include it into the batter if he'd want it be uniform.

Just throw in some rainbow sprinkles and stir.

Fill a cake pan with the batter.

Bake as directed on the packet.

After the cake has cooled, you may assist your kid ice it.

If desired, additional embellishments may be added with icing tubes and other similar tools.

Ready, set, serve!

You may also bake some delicious treats like cookies and brownies.

Use extra caution around the stove and other hot appliances while your youngster is around.

IDENTICAL AND DISTINCT

You should test your child's ability to recognize similarities and differences. You may discover out by playing the game "Same and Different."

Materials and Tools:

Images of individuals that appear alike Images of animals, buildings, cuisines, and other things that are similar yet distinct Place them on a table or floor

Instructions with necessary skills:

Choose a wide range of images, including those of your family if you can.

Place two photos of comparable people, homes, animals, etc., on the floor or table in front of your youngster.

Inquire of him the similarities between the images.

Inquire of him the differences.

If help is needed, provide it.

Relate what he said in response.

For the other images, please follow the same procedure.

Alternate version: put up a photo exhibit of your extended family and discuss the ways in which they are alike and different. Describe the precise ways in which your kid is like other children while also

what makes him unique and distinct from his siblings and cousins.

Careful comparisons of siblings are necessary to prevent the development of feelings of inferiority or jealousy in your youngster.

PROGRESS MARKERS

Even if the "stones" are really paper plates, it's still pleasant to walk down a path made of them.

Materials and Tools:

Pen and paper

Instructions with necessary skills:

The paper plates should be numbered.

The plates should be arranged in numbered sequence along a route through the home or yard. Keep them at least as far apart as a child's step would be.

Include some unusual detours along the way, such crossing a chair, jumping over a cushion, or crawling beneath a table.

Take your kid on a numbered paper plate adventure.

Restart the game and make a fresh configuration of the plates to follow.

Put the plates farther apart for a more difficult game. Follow the trail and pick up the plates with your kid.

Make sure your toddler doesn't get wounded attempting to reach a dish by being led in the wrong direction.

ADHESIVE TAPE

Just a roll of tape may provide hours of entertainment while teaching your youngster crucial life lessons.

Materials and Tools:

Scotch tape, masking tape, electrical tape, or any transparent or brightly colored tape roll (Avoid duct tape.)

Instructions with necessary skills:

Apply tape to your clothing and then wrap a lengthy piece of tape over your body in different places (and skin, if you like).

Start by saying hello and demonstrating your tape manipulation skills to your kid.

To get his assistance, giving him one end of the tape and ask him to pull the other end.

The youngster should slowly and carefully remove the tape from your body, bending and twisting as necessary.

And now, covering your infant with tape, try again. (Don't make contact with his skin.) 6. Allow your kid to free himself from the tape by pulling on it.

Give it another try and this time let your youngster apply and then remove the tape from your body while they play.

Optional twist: tape a trail through the home and have your kid follow it, removing tape as he goes.

Warning: Make sure the tape doesn't become stuck on your kid's skin.

THE TEA PARTY MOVEMENT

Throw your kid a tea party in the afternoon so you can all share a sweet treat.

Materials and Tools:

The fixings for a tea party, including the teapot, teacups, tablecloth, China, and nice silverware, plus a selection of tea-time treats like cookies and miniature sandwiches, are as essential as the beverage of choice.

Instructions with necessary skills:

Usual the table for the tea party with your finest China and a tablecloth.

Create some tea, juice, or water and put it in the teapot.

Relax with some tea and cookies while catching up with each other.

Together, you should clean up the mess and schedule next week's tea party.

Another option is to meet for breakfast or lunch on a particular occasion.

Just a word of warning: the tea shouldn't be served too hot. Tea may not be the preferred beverage for your youngster, so feel free to substitute juice or another drink.

RELEASE AND CALL
Your child's coordination and other abilities will benefit greatly from this exercise.

Materials and Tools:

Rubber ball of moderate size Vast wilderness

Instructions with necessary skills:

Look pick a ball that is manageable in size for your kid to catch.

Practicing this in the great outdoors is best, but any open area will do.

Consider a broad class, like playthings or food.

Ask your kid to come up with some instances that fit the description.

Get started with some back-and-forth ball throwing.

Each player who catches the ball has to name an item that falls within the designated category.

If a player fumbles the ball, you may always start again with a new set of rules.

Play the game sitting on the floor with your legs apart and roll the ball back and forth while reciting an example from the category whenever you pass the ball.

Avoid damaging anything when playing in a public space. Softly toss the ball.

CLAY FIGURES
With some sidewalk chalk, you may assist your youngster imagine themselves as a superhero, a princess, a humorous monster, and so on.

Materials and Tools:

Sidewalk or driveway Colored chalk Sunny day

Instructions with necessary skills:

Take some sidewalk chalk and enjoy the sunshine.

A fun action to do with your kid is to create a silhouette of her on the sidewalk.

Enable her to fill in the outline with more detail by using various colored chalks.

Help her visualize a magnificent being she can construct from the blueprint, whether it's a superhero, princess, monster, etc.

Allow her to create as many chalk figures as she wants.

Alternately, when the sun isn't shining, you may have your kid lay on the pavement while you sketch a silhouette of her body.

Be cautious not to leave any sharp objects or shards of glass lying about.

FANCY DRESS
Look at your kid as he puts on some nice clothes and becomes a whole new person!

Materials and Tools:

Clothing items from a local thrift shop that may be worn for role playing, such as dresses, skirts, jumpers, trousers, shirts, belts, jackets, coats, vests, shoes, hats, gloves, jewelry, scarves, and so on.

Instructions with necessary skills:

Get a bunch of different outfits and store them in a big box for pretend play.

The box should be placed in the middle of the play area and the kid should be allowed to take it out and explore it.

Put him to work putting together an outfit by exploring the garments and accessories available.

When he is fully clothed, inquire as to his identity and his plans. He has to start living as his new self.

Your youngster should be allowed to wear the garments for a short time before being allowed to switch to something else.

Change it up by having your kid act out a play for one. One alternative is to have him bring a buddy over and have them both do a skit.

Be careful not to put any pins or other sharp objects inside the box with your garments.

BEAT OUT A HYMN
Do you know whether your kid can do a chant-chant-chant on the drums? A simple beat-beat-beat is all that's needed. Sing and chant along with the drums!

Materials and Tools:

at least 2 drums or other percussion instruments

Instructions with necessary skills:

One of you should drum while the other watches, so go out and buy or manufacture two drums. Another surface, such as a tabletop, might be used instead.

Use a rhythmic tapping pattern, such as tap-tap-tap, on the drum.

Instruct your kiddo to play her drum in time with the beat.

Once she's got the beat down, have her add some vocals. You may say, "My name is Jane" while you drum tap-tap-tap-tap.

Keep making up drum beats and chants, switching up the tempo and the lyrics whenever you want. The other individual should follow your lead.

Rotate who gets to be the model for the other.

You might even have a "conversation" in which one person talks while the other person drums in time with their words. Drum and talk to each other.

Watch out that your kid doesn't damage her fingers by drumming too vigorously. If your kid is getting lost in the music, just take it down a notch.

HINT, HINT, LOCATE THE CLOCK

In a few of minutes, your kid has to locate the chiming timepiece. Whence might it come? There has to be a lot additional hearing on her part.

Materials and Tools:

Alarm clock or timer with a distinct ticking sound

Instructions with necessary skills:

Put an alarm or timer in a concealed location within or outside the home.

Get your kid in there and make them listen.

The alarm will go off in three minutes, so give your kid a chance to locate the clock. She has to pay close attention to the sound of the clock and go in that direction.

If she is struggling, offer her some pointers.

You may play again, but this time have your kid search for the clock even faster.

Help your kid locate the clock by describing her progress as "hot" or "cold" as she nears or recedes from the object.

Be careful not to put the clock in a dangerous area, and be sure to praise your youngster for his or her accomplishments.

WHATCHAMACALLIT!

Your kid will have fun envisioning the functions of strange-looking new things and giving them made-up names. The more outlandish, the better.

Materials and Tools:

Paper bag A variety of strange household items that your kid has never seen before, like a garlic press, nose-hair plucked, beach shell, pizza cutter, hose nozzle, vacuum attachment, eyelash curler, and so on

Instructions with necessary skills:

Put everything in a paper bag and place it down in the middle of you and the kid.

Let your kid pick out something.

Get him to come up with a clever name for it.

Have your youngster visualize the item's function and tell you about it.

Put the next item back in his hands and have him do it again.

Don't stop playing until he has named and described everything.

Alternately, instead of asking your kid to explain the item's purpose in words, have him mimic the item's operation while you attempt to decipher his meaning!

Take care, you need to make sure they're safe to touch.

PLAY DOUGH THAT DOESN'T HAVE TO BE THROWN AWAY

Put this play dough in your kid's hands so he or she may have fun with it, make some decorations, and then eat them!

Materials and Tools:

Gingerbread, either homemade or purchased at a store; table sprinkles; cookie cutters; rolling pin; plastic knife; fork; cookie sheet; oven

Instructions with necessary skills:

Prepare a batch of your go-to gingerbread dough. If the dough seems too moist, work in some additional flour until it reaches a play dough consistency. If it's too dry, just add water.

Place the dough in a bowl.

Allow your kid to use the tools of his choice to mold the dough into figures, animals, or anything else he can imagine.

Encourage him to use sprinkles and candy pieces to adorn the shapes.

Upon his completion, spread the things out on a baking sheet and bake them as directed.

Prepare, let cool, and enjoy!

Alternatively, you may bake gingerbread cookies and use pre-made frosting to give them a festive look before serving them as a snack.

Warning: Please supervise your youngster carefully while they are near a hot oven.

The dough tools are secure for use. Make sure your kid doesn't consume any of the dough if it includes raw eggs.

POSE POSTURE

Your kid will have a blast creating a Foot Face sock puppet.

Materials and Tools:

Items needed include: a sock that has been recently washed; a piece of cardboard; scissors; permanent felt-tip pens; yarn; buttons; a needle and thread; and any other embellishments (optional)

Instructions with necessary skills:

Get a clean sock that's around the same size as your kid.

Use a craft knife to cut a cardboard form only slightly bigger than the sock.

Put the sock on the cardboard and stretch it out.

Use permanent felt-tip pens to have your youngster design a crazy face towards the toe end of the sock. If she needs your help, sketch with her.

Create the mouth's base close to the sock's heel.

To illustrate this, please add a tongue and set of teeth to the relevant mouth.

You may embellish it as you wish by sewing on yarn hair, button eyes, etc.

Take the sock out of the cardboard and put it on your kid's hand.

Let her communicate for the puppet while she opens and closes her hand to give it expression.

To switch things up, have your kid put on a puppet performance using two sock puppets, one for each hand.

Keep an eye on how the permanent felt-tip pens are being used. Make sure any embellishments you sew on are well-anchored.

GEOMAGNETIC SEARCH

Now for a scientifically enlightening treasure hunt of a different kind! Give your kid a magnet and see what he or she can find that sticks to it!

Materials and Tools:

Magnet that is age-appropriate for kids.

Instructions with necessary skills:

Get a kid-friendly magnet from a shop selling toys or school supplies, or borrow one from a friend who has one. You should look for a magnet that is strong enough to hold its but not too strong for your toddler to handle safely.

Use a few test objects to show how the magnet works.

Get your kid to go on a hunt for magnets throughout the home.

After he's tried a few things, have him take a go at predicting whether or not anything will attach to the magnet.

Tell him to keep searching for magnetic riches. Be sure to keep an eye on any experiments he plans on doing.

When he's done, have him discuss the commonalities he saw between the magnetic objects.

Another option is to gather a variety of household things and display them on a table. Involve your kid in figuring out which ones are magnets. Toss the things into magnetic and non-magnetic heaps after he tests them.

Caution: Be sure the products he checks are safe to touch.

FORM WALK

Your toddler will have a great time learning her shapes while you take her on a stroll around the home or outdoors.

Materials and Tools:

Geometrically rich region

Instructions with necessary skills:

On your stroll, point out various shapes to your youngster, such as a circle, square, triangle, rectangle, oval, and so on.

Explore the home, yard, park, or surrounding area by strolling about.

Pick a shape and have her count how many things in the room share it.

As soon as she has found five, she should switch to a new form and continue searching.

Until she has found all the shapes, keep looking.

After you're done, invite her to have a snack with you and see if you can guess the form of her cracker, cookie, or sandwich.

To switch things up, bring a pad of paper with you on your stroll and have your kid sketch the item every time she sees a form.

Warning: She's trying to keep track of all those shapes, so be careful she doesn't slip and fall!

POWERFUL PIECES

To help your young child develop creativity and motor skills, you can recycle milk cartons into blocks. Every time a box is emptied, she can add to her collection!

Materials and Tools:

Supplies: (1, 2, 3, and 5 gallon) milk cartons; scissors; a pen or pencil; a ruler; duct tape; decorative contact paper, stickers, oil paint, and paintbrushes;

Instructions with necessary skills:

The milk cartons' tops should be lopped off.

Please clean the cartons by rinsing and drying them.

Take a width measurement across the bottom of the first carton.

From the lower corners, mark this same distance up.

Start cutting from the top corners and stop at the marks.

If you want to compact the carton, fold the top flaps in and secure them with duct tape to create a cube.

The cube may be painted with oil-based paint, covered with ornamental contact paper and stickers, or both.

It should be repeated with the remaining cartons. After the blocks have been prepared, your youngster may play by stacking, constructing, and knocking them down.

For a twist, have your kid pitch in and help you build the blocks.

Caution: Please use extreme caution while handling sharp objects and paint near your youngster.

CURIOUS BOX

Kiddos like a good mystery. Conceal anything surprising inside of a plain box to create an exciting surprise!

Materials and Tools:

You will need: a paper bag a small box, like a shoebox, and tape a number of objects that are meaningful to your kid, such as his shoe, toy, doll, unique cup, favorite book, and so on.

Instructions with necessary skills:

Get a paper bag and put in it many child-friendly objects that he or she would recognize but can't see.

Give your kid a bag, tell him to shut his eyes, and have him choose anything out of it to put in the box.

Keep your toddler occupied by closing the lid and taping the box shut.

Describe the contents as a mystery and give him a hint.

Give him time to mull it over by holding and shaking the package.

Let him guess what it is by providing him with a hint.

Don't stop providing him hints until he properly identifies the object.

You may play again when you open the box and see what's inside.

Let your kid take a turn concealing thing in the box and guessing what they are!

Take care to ensure that everything you touch is secure and safe.

HANG A NECKLACE

Give your youngster a few macaroni noodles and some thread and let him create his necklace.

Materials and Tools:

You'll need: 8 bowls Red, blue, green, and yellow food coloring 4 spoons for stirring Small, straight macaroni noodles Paper towels String Big, dull yarn needle

Instructions with necessary skills:

Put four bowls on the table and add a few drops of food coloring to each bowl.

Scoop the noodles into four separate heaps and serve them accordingly. If you're using macaroni, make sure it's the straight kind and not the bent kind.

The noodles should be stirred until they are evenly colored.

The excess dye may be removed by pouring the noodles onto a paper towel.

After the noodles have dried, divide them into four bowls.

Provide your youngster with some thread so they may fashion a necklace.

Attach a single macaroni noodle to a thread.

Use the other end to thread a big needle.

Give your kid a needle and some thread, and let him or her fill the string with macaroni noodles.

Put the necklace around his neck and tie the ends together.

Substitute colorful cereals with holes for the macaroni.

Warning: Caution should be used while instructing a kid in the use of a big needle. It's important that the necklace is long enough to go over your kid's head.

EXHIBITION WITH PICTURES

Looking at old photographs might bring back fond childhood memories. Play a game of "Put the pictures in order of when they were taken" with your kid.

Materials and Tools:

Table Include 3 or 4 photographs depicting a memorable family outing, celebration, or event in your child's life, such as a trip, a birthday, or a special occasion.

Instructions with necessary skills:

Randomly shuffle and scatter the pictures around a table.

Challenge your kid's memory by having her choose the picture that corresponds with the order in which events occurred.

Next, have her choose the picture that best depicts what occurred.

Keep going until she has chosen all the pictures and put them in order of when they were taken.

You may assist her recall additional specifics by asking her to recount the event from beginning to finish.

Another option is to give her a pile of images from different occasions and have her categorize them by kind of function. The next step is to have her arrange the events in time order.

Warn your kid to be gentle with the pictures, or make duplicates so she may use them.

PICTURE PUZZLE

Your kid will enjoy making his puzzle just as much as he enjoys putting together one. Pick a photo that he'll really be interested in seeing.

Materials and Tools:

Poster board Spray adhesive Black felt-tip pen Scissors Small box Table Interesting picture of family member, beloved animal, cartoon figure, etc.

Instructions with necessary skills:

Select a photograph that captures your attention.

Paint adhesive onto the poster board.

The image may be pressed into the sprayed surface and left there until it dries.

Create some easy puzzle lines on the image by drawing using a black felt-tip pen.

Use this guide for cutting out the image into puzzle pieces.

Collect the parts and store them in a handy container.

Place the package on the table and sit down with your kid to open it.

Tell him to remove the puzzle from its packaging, unload the components, and assemble it.

Give him hints if you think he'll need them so he can figure it out on his .

Have him describe what he sees after the image is finished.

Alternately, you may enlist his assistance in creating the puzzle from scratch before setting it aside for him to assemble.

You should use caution while working with spray adhesive and scissors in the presence of your kid, and always provide enough ventilation.

COLLAPSING TOWER

Oftentimes, children take more delight in destroying things than they do in constructing them. Here's an exciting construction game that ends with a twist!

Materials and Tools:

Blocks, crackers, or other stacked things Uncarpeted floor or big table

Instructions with necessary skills:

Seek for a level playing field, such as a big table or an area of the floor that is not carpeted.

Gather a number of thin, flat, and stackable objects, like blocks or crackers.

Build a tower by taking turns stacking the objects.

Teach your youngster the importance of taking care as the tower they are building rises in height.

Whoever causes the skyscraper to collapse is responsible for picking up the fragments.

Repeat that game!

Alternately, you might make or purchase a stacking game in which players take it in turns removing components from a tower in an effort to prevent it from tumbling over.

Be careful that your youngster won't be wounded if any of the things fall.

ROUGH CUT

If your kid likes to sketch, get a black surface and show her how her masterpieces may suddenly come to life in full color!

Materials and Tools:

Poster board (or other sturdy paper), scissors, crayons, black poster paint, a paintbrush, a paper clip, and a turkey skewer.

Instructions with necessary skills:

Reduce a piece of poster board to a square approximately 4 inches on each side.

Have your kid use a variety of crayons to fill in the whole thing. You should encourage her to color with a heavy hand.

Then, have her use black poster paint to cover the whole thing up. Let the paint dry thoroughly.

Instruct your youngster to scratch a pattern over the black paint with an opened paper clip or turkey skewer.

Seeing the pattern materialize in full color will astound her.

Alternative: swap out the regular Crayola felt-tip markers with the interchangeable ones. Encourage your youngster to create a picture with one color of marker, then alter the color by drawing over it with another.

Caution: Make sure your kid knows how to properly handle knives and other cutting tools.

MODIFICATION OF FORM

Your kid at this age can probably bend into any form you can imagine. Check out the variety of forms he can create!

Materials and Tools:

Rope long enough to span your kid's height (measured from his toes to his fingers) Scissors Clearance from furniture

Instructions with necessary skills:

Get your kid to stand as tall as possible, and then cut a rope to that length.

Remove anything that could be in the way on the ground or the grass.

Have your kid lay down on top of the rope that you've laid out in a straight line.

Make a bend in the rope and have your kid lay on top of it so that they're both in the same position.

Rotate the rope to form a new pattern for your youngster to follow, such as a S curve, V shape, wavy line, circle, triangle, square, etc.

Alternately, have your kid imagine the shapes he wants to create with the rope and then see if he can move his body to produce them. Alternatively, have him try to create all 26 letters of the alphabet with the rope.

Warning: make sure the ground is safe and clean for him to rest on.

BURST-AND-FALL DANCING

Listening to upbeat music and moving to the rhythm is a breeze. And yet, can your kid come to a halt when the music stops all of a sudden?

Materials and Tools:

Playing a tape or CD with dance music on a cassette player

Instructions with necessary skills:

Listen to some upbeat dancing music on a cassette or CD.

Make your kid wait in the center of the room for the music to start as they stand there.

When you hit "play," your kid should immediately begin to move.

When you press "stop," she has to freeze until the music starts up again.

Don't stop playing and starting up again till the song is done.

Replace the current track with another one, or try a new genre of music.

Make it interesting by instructing your kid to switch up her dance moves every time the music stops and starts up again. One alternative is to let her take turns pausing and restarting the music as you move.

Take care to cleanse the area of any potential hazards.

HAIRDRESSER'S & COSMETICIAN'S WORKSHOP

Get your kid a haircut at the Styling Salon - in the comfort of your tub! You can get your kid cleaned up and dressed up at the same time!

Materials and Tools:

Toys for the kids: a bathtub, a food coloring set, hair clips, and a mirror that can't be

Instructions with necessary skills:

Prepare a hot bath by filling the tub.

Tell your kid to go in there.

To produce colored suds, pour a tiny quantity of shampoo into your palm and add a few drops of food coloring (it rinses out easily).

Apply a generous amount of shampoo and massage it into your child's scalp.

Let your kid take a look at herself in the mirror.

Give her some colored shampoo and let her experiment with new hairdos.

For more merriment, try with various hair clips and other hair holders.

Don't forget to text your trip with photos!

Remove the shampoo by rinsing well.

Make it more interesting by moussing your kid's hair before letting her experiment with various hairdos in the bath. Remove the mousse by shampooing as usual.

If you don't want your child's eyes to become irritated, use baby shampoo. A washcloth should be on ready to mop up any stray shampoo.

DISCOURSE AROUND THE TABLE

Here's a fun educational activity for the next time you're waiting for your food at a restaurant.

Materials and Tools:

Cutlery, plates, salt and pepper shakers, napkin holders, toothpicks, sugar packets, syrup, menus, and so on are just approximately of the things that may be found on a typical dining room table.

Instructions with necessary skills:

In order to occupy your child's mind while waiting for your food, you might pretend to ponder about anything on the table.

Just give him a hint about it, whether it's the color, the size, the weight, the purpose, etc.

Give him a chance to guess what it is.

Get excited when he succeeds!

If his guess is wrong, give him further hints.

After a successful guess, give him the opportunity to provide you hints by picking an item.

Keep taking rounds until there is nothing left to take.

Extend the game to use things from the restaurant itself for a twist on the classic version.

Take care to keep your youngster seated at the dinner table. Tell him he has to get up from his seat and find it.

TURN-BASED PHOTOGRAPH

Having a second opinion may be invaluable while trying to complete a complex project.

Materials and Tools:

A table timer, two pieces of paper, and crayons or felt-tip pens

Instructions with necessary skills:

Hand your kid a piece of paper and keep one for yourself.

Place yourself across from one another at a table and start sketching anything with the crayons or felt-tip pens.

You should start counting down from one minute.

When the buzzer sounds, swap sheets and keep working on your partner's image.

In order to complete taking images, reset the timer and do it again.

Give the images titles and place them up on the wall.

Alternatively, you and your partner might start by sketching the respective heads of an animal or human. After the head is done, switch sheets and begin sketching the bodies. Again, switch places and finish your drawings by adding arms, legs, tails, etc.

Caution: Only use felt-tip pens that aren't poisonous.

FIND A WAY TO CROSS THE ROOM WITHOUT BEING NOTICED

The suspense mounts as your little one sneak up behind you to take a toy.

Materials and Tools:

Whether it's a snack or a toy, it'

Instructions with necessary skills:

Place yourself in the center of a room, seated on the floor, with your back to the entrance.

Retain the kid out of the way and have them count to 10 while they wait.

Put something enjoyable, like a snack or a toy, behind your back.

At age 10, have your kid sneak into the room and attempt to get the food or toy before you catch her sneakily.

Just switch off each once in a while.

Put on a blindfold and put the thing in front of you as a variation. It's going to take some sneaking around on your kid's part to attempt and get that toy. Try to snag her every once in a while, when she reaches for the item!

Make sure the floor isn't too slick, and don't make sweeping motions with your arms that might hit your kid.

THE BALL IS IN THE BOWL

Here's a straightforward game that will entertain and test your kid.

Materials and Tools:

Space on the floor cleared off Small, non-bouncy ball One big bowl

Instructions with necessary skills:

Get rid of the clutter and set a bowl in the center of the floor as a play area.

Put the chair back a foot or two from the table so the kid can still reach the bowl.

Entrust her with the ball and instruct her to throw it into the container. Show it many times if you have to.

Have her back up a little after she makes a couple shots, then try again.

Instead of one large dish, choose a variety of bowls and arrange them throughout the room. Fill the bowls up with stickers and other incentives. Whenever your kid makes a basket, reward her with anything from the dish.

Avoid using any dishes made of glass. Instead of paper, try plastic or metal.

CONSTITUTION OF FRIENDS

It has been said that two brains are better than one. Is it preferable to have two bodies instead of one? Playing with your kid is a great way to find out!

Materials and Tools:

A spotless floor and two rolls of cellophane or colorful tape

Instructions with necessary skills:

Meet your youngster eye to eye in the midst of a clear space.

Give him one and retain the other if you only have two rolls of tape.

You should both get taped together, so tell him to start taping himself to you. Wrap by hand up from head to toe by tape, and any other places you can think of!

Then, in concert, find out how to traverse the space.

Play it safe by sticking to basic activities like picking up toys, picking up the phone, and playing simple games.

If you find yourself in a sticky situation and need to get out fast, have a pair of scissors close at hand. If it doesn't work, try passing along the tape remover after you're done playing.

Change it up by taping stiff cardboard to your kid's limbs and making him walk like Frankenstein.

Play on carpeted or grassy ground, and watch out for falling on top of your kid!

A SEARCH FOR BUGS

Your kid undoubtedly thinks bugs are cool right about now. Go on a Bug Hunt and have a good time with your friends.

Materials and Tools:

Yard, park, or other outside location Magnifying glass Bug identification book Pad of paper and felt-tip pens or Polaroid camera

Instructions with necessary skills:

Get out of the city and go to a park or a natural location on foot or by car. A tiny sketchbook and sketching implements, or a Polaroid camera, are useful to have on hand.

Take a stroll about the area and look for bugs with your kid. To inspect anything more closely, you should use the use of a magnifying lens.

If your kid comes across an insect, she may either draw a picture of it on her pad or snap a photo of it.

Keep exploring and seeking for more bugs along the way.

Once you have a substantial collection, you may go home and go through all the sketches and photographs. Have the film processed if you're using a conventional camera.

Get your kid to look at the bugs in the images or photos by laying them out on the table. Pose the question of what is the same and what is different, and have her investigate.

Have your kid use a bug book if you have one to see if they can number out what caring of bugs they are dealing with.

To change things up, try a Plant Hunt instead of the original game and see how many varieties of plants you can locate.

Be wary of stinging and biting insects!

PLEASE SHARE A SCUPTURE

Making a sculpture together is a great way to express your creativity and collaborate with others.

Materials and Tools:

Tabletop modeling compound, play dough, baker's clay, etc.

Instructions with necessary skills:

Toy clay and play dough may be purchased in a variety of colors, or you can easily create you .

Separate the dough into equal halves. The parent should split the item in two and give the kid the other half.

Make a little sculpture to start with and put it on a table.

Get your kid to shape a little bit and then add it to your creation.

Collaborate with each other to build up the sculpture. Take in the transformation as you put in the effort.

When you've finished using all the dough, stand back and take a look at your creation before deciding on a name for it as a group.

You might also try letting your kid make his sculpture in parallel with yours. Swap places with someone after a few minutes. While you're busy with his sculpture, have him work on yours. Keep working on the sculptures until you're done.

It's important to sculpt safely, so don't use anything hazardous.

CONVERSATIONS ON THE PHONE

Talking over the phone might be more enjoyable than meeting in person at times. Toy mobile phones are easy to make, and you and your kid will have a blast pretending to talk on them.

Materials and Tools:

Stick-on objects, such as printed contact paper, spray paint, stickers, or other similar items Two tiny rectangular boxes, such as candy boxes, long enough to fit from your child's ear to his mouth Scissors

Instructions with necessary skills:

Create two mobile phones by spray painting or coating narrow rectangular boxes with colored contact paper.

Create an opening for your ear at the top and a slit for your mouth at the bottom on the same side.

You should give your kid the mobile phone and allow him put stickers and other things on it.

Contact him through mobile phone by crossing the room or by asking him to contact you.

Get together and talk about anything is on your mind!

You don't have to really switch on the real mobile phones if you're just going to play with the pretend ones.

Warn: make sure there are no sharp corners.

CONTOURING THE FACE

Give your youngster a new item to admire when he looks in the mirror; he's learning to take pride in his appearance.

Materials and Tools:

Paints or crayons for coloring faces (nontoxic options may be found at art supply or toy shops) Tabletop or floor mirror

Instructions with necessary skills:

Lay down a table or the floor and set out the face paints.

Put a mirror within sight so your kid may check his progress.

Indulge his creativity and let him paint his face.

Take photographs, go to the neighbors, or terrify the family after he's done!

Make him invent a backstory to fit the new appearance. Let him put on a little performance if he wants to.

Alternately, paint your kid's face blindfolded. When he appearances in the mirror, he will be taken aback. Find out how he makes each of the portraits unique by inquiring about the differences in the faces he paints.

Warning: Only use safe, easily-removable face paints.

IT'S NO SECRET THAT EXPRESSIONS ON PEOPLE'S FACES CONVEY EMOTION.

She feels many different things, but your kid doesn't always know how to talk about it. Here's a game that will help.

Materials and Tools:

cheap photo books or magazines with pictures of individuals showing their feelings Scissors A flat surface

Instructions with necessary skills:

Gather some photographs of kids and adults showing their feelings via facial expressions.

83

Prepare a stack of cut-out photos.

Put the photos, facedown, between you and your kid while sitting on the floor or at a table.

If you want to display the first photo to your kid, you should flip it over.

Just ask her how she thinks the other person is feeling. If she is having trouble communicating, you may want to help her out by giving her some vocabulary terms.

Get her to make a face like the one in the photo.

Share your thoughts on the value of expressing a wide range of feelings with her.

Pick an image from the stack in secret one at a time.

person. Make a face like the one in the photo, and your opponent must identify what you're feeling.

Caution: When using scissors, cut images carefully.

JOKINGLY USE OF FOIL

Kids have a blast playing "guess what it is" games, particularly when the objects up for identification are amusing or common.

Materials and Tools:

Aluminum foil Paper bag A selection of your kid's smaller toys (dolls, blocks, balls, dolls, plush animals, etc.) a table or the floor

Instructions with necessary skills:

Gather a wide selection of your kid's smaller playthings.

Cover each item with aluminum foil.

Put everything in a paper bag and put it somewhere in the middle of you and your kid, either on the floor or a table.

Request that your youngster shut his eyes.

Give him just one of those things you brought out.

Tell him to run his hands over it and see if he can figure out what it is.

Unwrap the object after he makes a guess to see whether he was correct.

Keep going until everything has been named.

Give your kid an accidental to show off their wrapping skills by having you guess what they've wrapped.

Change things up by substituting related objects, such

when used as toys or stuffed animals. For your child's sake, try to make it more difficult for them to tell the objects apart.

Take care that anything you're wrapping isn't dangerous to touch.

PLANNING A TRIP TO THE SHOESHOPS

When your shoes have a good fit, you won't even notice you're walking. The shaky steps of a child's first steps may be turned into a game of shoe shopping.

Materials and Tools:

Heels, boots, shoes, slippers, sneakers, and other men's and women's and men's footwear.

Instructions with necessary skills:

Collect a wide selection of footwear from your closets, or browse for bargains at secondhand stores.

Lay out the footwear for your kid to "shop" for.

Enable him to try on a pair of shoes of his choosing.

Try them out by having him take a stroll around the home.

Put him in the shoes and have him do something, like step over a cushion or crawl under a table.

Have him choose another pair to wear after he's done with the first.

Shoe-matching: the art of making walking even more difficult than it really is.

Make sure the ground is clear and don't give him anything to wear that might cause him to twist his ankle. Keep a near eye on him while he attempts the wobbly walk.

FORMING A PLATE AND A CUP FROM PAPER

Demonstrate to your kid that he can use everything he finds lying around to make something cool. See how he can use paper plates and cups as a starting point.

Materials and Tools:

Paper plates of many sizes and colors Paper cups of varying colors Smooth floor or cleared table Tape or glue Popsicle sticks (optional)

Instructions with necessary skills:

Paper plates and glasses should be set out on a flat floor or cleared table.

Encourage your youngster's creativity by having him or her use the plates and cups to construct something.

If he needs help getting started, provide suggestions or demonstrate how to alternate stacking the plates and cups.

Don't leave him hanging by not providing him with the means to secure the items together.

Provide supplementary constructable besides Popsicle sticks for kids to play with.

Alternative: Join forces with others in a joint construction venture.

Warning: Make sure he knows how to safely use the tape and glue.

PROCEED IN THE PATH SET BY THE LEADING INSTITUTION

Rotate who is in charge. The follower must mimic your every action as you make your way around the home or yard.

Materials and Tools:

Room for a lot

Instructions with necessary skills:

Figure out who will be in charge initially.

One person acts as the leader and walks about the home or yard in any pattern she chooses, while the other person mimics her every step.

Alternate who is in charge at regular intervals.

Substitute music as background noise to get the creative juices flowing. You may even take your game to a local park or gym to play.

Care must be taken to ensure the safety of both the leader and the group's followers. Keep a close eye on your kid to make sure she doesn't do any risky stunts.

FLIES AND GRASSHOPERS

In this entertaining activity, your kid will learn the importance of paying attention and following instructions.

Materials and Tools:

Cleared the space with posters of flying insects like grasshoppers and butterflies.

Instructions with necessary skills:

Insect illustrations may be found in a variety of nature books and periodicals.

Let's have a chat about the various insects and their modes of movement. When in doubt, provide a demonstration.

Raise your stance in the center of the empty space.

To start, you should yell the name of the first bug you see, such as "Grasshopper!"

You and your partner should bounce about like a grasshopper to mimic the insect's behavior.

If you and your partner are silent for more than a few seconds, you must then yell out an insect's name, such as "Butterfly!"

You and your partner must immediately adopt the fluidity of a butterfly's flight.

Switch up your routine by taking turns pointing out bugs in the images you view and adapting to the new poses.

You might also try to mimic the behaviors of other creatures, such as reptiles and mammals.

motions.

Care must be taken to provide enough space for safe and comfortable movement in all directions.

WITHIN MY WALLET

Children are naturally fascinated about the contents of your briefcase or handbag, so feel free to open it up and share the contents with them.

Materials and Tools:

Floor or table Contents of bag or briefcase

Instructions with necessary skills:

Take away everything your kid couldn't possibly use or may get hurt from.

Place an item of furniture (such a briefcase or pocketbook) between you and your kid and sit down.

Inquire as to her thoughts on the contents of the bag or briefcase.

Take out your keys, wallet, Kleenex, and so on as she calls them out.

Find out from her whether she is familiar with the products and what they are used for.

If she is struggling to come up with what to bring, you may offer her hints by amplification what each item is used for.

Another option is to have your kid stuff a bag or a handbag with of random objects and see if you can guess what's inside. In case you need more hints, you can always ask her.

Be careful to get rid of anything that might be harmful or improper.

BRING IN SOME DRILLS

This entertaining activity will simultaneously help your kid improve her memory and motor abilities.

Materials and Tools:

Big, wide-open area

Instructions with necessary skills:

Get everyone out into the open and play the game.

Go ahead and face each other in the center of the room.

You may get started by just moving one body component. Raise your arm as an illustration.

Get your kid to mimic your actions.

Expand the first action by adding another one. Both actions, in the same sequence, should be repeated by your youngster.

Increase the number of actions until she forgets them all.

Let your kid take turns coming up with a dance routine you have to copy. Let her start with one step and keep piling on more until everyone has forgotten what she's doing.

A new twist on the game is to use just words, rather than physical motions.

Be careful not to run into anything, and make sure the path is clear.

EFFECTIVE WAND OF MAGIC

Is your kid aware that he has a miraculous body? Simply hand him a magic wand, and he'll demonstrate its capabilities.

Materials and Tools:

A magic wand is a dowel or stick between one and two feet long that has been decorated with colorful ribbons or painted in a rainbow of hues.

Instructions with necessary skills:

Place yourself on seats that face each other.

Tell your kid you can do miracles with his body because you have a magic wand.

Put the wand's tip in your kid's hand.

Then, have him show you all the amazing things his hand can do, like wave, grip, wriggle, open, shut, stretch, point, play the piano, and so on.

Continue stroking the rest of his body with the wand, such as his hands, feet, arms, legs, chest, head, fingers, toes, lips, shoulders, knees, etc.

Change things up by taking turns showing off your body's abilities with the wand.

It would be wise to avoid poking each other inadvertently.

COURSE OF OBSTACLES

Children, eager to test their growing physical abilities, are always up for a new adventure. They also seem to like obstacle courses endlessly.

Materials and Tools:

Pillows and cushions, blankets and sheets, huge cardboard boxes, seats and tables, bowls, buckets, baskets, tires, inner tubes, hoops, ropes, soft toys, and blocks fill a vast room.

Instructions with necessary skills:

Gather a number of objects that your kid can try to jump, crawl, or roll over, under, around, or through.

Linearly place the objects.

Send your kid out at the beginning of the lesson and encourage her to see it through to the conclusion if she can.

See how she handles the obstacles she encounters and give her kudos when she succeeds!

Permit her to create a maze of challenges for you.

Avoid using anything sharp or breakable, and make sure your youngster understands how to use anything.

SCULPTURES OF PIPE CLEANERS

If you want to assist your kid improve her hand dexterity, try this enjoyable exercise.

Materials and Tools:

Colorful pipe cleaners for the table

Instructions with necessary skills:

Organize a workspace for your kid by clearing the table.

Place the pipe cleaners in a convenient location.

Guide her through the steps of manipulating the pipe cleaners with her fingers to get the desired results.

Just let her create anything she likes. If she's having problems getting started, provide suggestions like animals, people, letters, numbers, structures, freeform sculptures, and so on.

Alternate version: Collaborate with your youngster on ambitious projects like constructing a zoo, a town with buildings and people, a large family, etc.

For their safety, remind your youngster that the ends of the pipe cleaners are pointy.

STUPID PROMENADES

Play a game of Silly Walks with your kid now that she understands all there is to know about walking!

Materials and Tools:

Extensive room for recreation

Instructions with necessary skills:

Locate a large location that will provide enough opportunity for exploration and innovation.

One player begins by coming up with an absurd walking pattern, such as rubber legs, one foot forward/one foot backward, walking on one's knees, walking with one's legs spread wide apart, walking on one's heels, walking toe-to-heel, and so forth.

Create ridiculous dances and make your partner mimic you.

Besides crazy walks, you may also come up with other ridiculous physical gestures. Inspire your kid to use her complete self in her imaginative play.

Avoid potential danger by removing any obstructions.

POSSIBLY ODOROUS MATERIALS

As he develops and learns more about the world around him, your child's ability to identify and appreciate different aromas will improve. He will like playing with Odorous Items.

Materials and Tools:

Paper bag filled with various fragrant objects like a banana, coffee, fresh bread, flower, perfume, rubber, teddy bear, etc.

Floor or table?

Instructions with necessary skills:

Gather all the smelly things you can find and put them in individual paper bags.

Put the paper bags in the middle of a table or the floor and sit down with your kid there.

Hold one of the bags up to his face so that he can't see what's inside.

Get him to try to identify a scent.

If he's struggling, offer him some pointers.

When he makes the right guess, reveal the object.

It is essential to repeat this process until each bag has been opened and scented.

Try a variant by choosing foods with comparable aromas and seeing whether your kid can identify the difference.

Take care that the scents aren't overpowering.

INVESTIGATE THIS PERSON AS THAT UNIQUE SOLUTION

This is another entertaining guessing game that your kid will like. Give her a hint about a particular someone in your life and see if she can figure it out. It may very well be her.

Materials and Tools:

Photos of loved ones, acquaintances, and icons from many walks of life

Instructions with necessary skills:

Collect photos of individuals you know and place them in a group.

Make your kid check out the photographs.

Let her know she's on your mind by mentioning a loved one. She must resort to yes/no questions to determine who it is. Offer some examples of questions to be asked if that is required.

You should grill her until she identifies the VIP.

Have her picture someone wonderful as you ask her yes/no questions.

Remove the images off the table before she starts asking questions for an added challenge.

For your child's sanity, it's best to stick with folks she already knows.

BARBECUE WITH TEDDY BEARS

Even during a Teddy Bear Picnic, your kid will pick up a ton of useful knowledge from all the different games and exercises they'll do.

Materials and Tools:

Pack a picnic including: a couple of stuffed animals; a picnic basket; a blanket; a variety of sandwiches; beverages; cookies; and other snacks;

Instructions with necessary skills:

Make a picnic out of it by telling your child's stuffed animals they're going on a picnic.

Collectively make sandwiches, snacks, and beverages.

Create a picnic basket with the food. A picnic blanket should be among the items you bring.

Take your picnic basket and stuffed animals for a stroll in the park. Have a wonderful meal and a lively discussion, and don't forget to engage the bears in on the fun!

Have a sinch in the family room and act like you're in the woods as an alternative to going to the park.

Warning: Make sure your kid knows how to properly pack food so it doesn't go bad while camping.

FOOT-DRAPER

The aim of this exercise is that it challenges your coordination skills. In order for your kid to express herself freely, she will need to tap as she speaks.

Materials and Tools:

Two sets of floor-tapping footwear, one for you and one for your kid; two chairs

Instructions with necessary skills:

Sit your kid down in a low enough chair so she can put her feet on the floor.

Equip her feet with some tap shoes.

Tap your feet together and sit in a chair directly across from her.

Pick anything to talk about, such that you have planned for tomorrow, what occurred today, or what you want to accomplish this weekend.

Alternate who speaks. However, you'll need to touch each word as you say it. Saying, "I want to go to the park," while simultaneously tapping out each phrase, will result in the desired action. Get your youngster to emphasis certain phrases by tapping them harder.

Keep talking till your feet and tongues hurt!

Put on some thimbles and tap the table with your words for a variant.

Be careful that your kid doesn't hurt himself by putting his foot on the furniture.

teeter and totter as you attempt to tap out her words.

NOSE BREAKERS

Your kid will enjoy tongue twisters at a time when her linguistic abilities are blossoming.

Materials and Tools:

Tongue Twisters: A Book for Kids

Instructions with necessary skills:

Find a book of easy tongue twisters that is appropriate for your child's reading level and check it out from the library or a bookshop.

Repeat reading a tongue-twister as slowly as possible. Consider, as examples, "She sells seashells on the seaside" and "A boisterous noise bothers an oyster."

Try saying it with your kid.

Then, you should hear her attempt it on her . Help her get through the whole statement without stumbling.

If she makes any amusing gaffes, you should laugh at them with her. Just kidding!

Optional twist: come up with your tongue twisters via cooperative effort.

Use caution while picking out twisters for your youngster; you don't want them to become angry or unhappy.

SHORT STORY

Here's an entertaining approach to make up a tale: just choose a different plaything and watch the plot shift!

Materials and Tools:

A paper bag Six to ten of your kid's toys, such a ball, doll, block, action figure, Lego piece, jigsaw, paintbrush, automobile, and so on

Instructions with necessary skills:

Wrap the toys up in a paper bag so your kid can't see them.

Put the bag in the middle of where you're sitting, whether it's on the floor or a table, and talk to your kid that way.

Here's one idea: grab a toy from the drawer and start telling a tale centered around it. If you use a ball as your prop, you may begin your tale by describing how it "once upon a time" bounced so high that it "reached the sky!" "

Bring out a different toy and have your youngster finish the narrative with it. The ball fell to the ground and hit a block, and the block exclaimed, "I wish I could bounce like you!" "'

Keep taking it in turns to shuffle the toys about and rewrite the tale to accommodate them.

When you get to the last toy, stop telling the narrative.

You may switch things up by playing the same game with products from other categories, such as food, clothes, plush animals, etc.

Take care, you need to make sure they're safe to handle.

MUSICAL WATERS

By getting creative with water instruments, show your kid that water isn't only for drinking and bathing.

Materials and Tools:

You'll need: a table, a pitcher of water, food coloring (if desired), and a metal spoon.

Instructions with necessary skills:

Place the wine glasses on a table.

Fill the first glass about an inch high with water.

To the other cups, add water until it is about half an inch higher than the first.

Drops of food coloring may be added to each glass for more entertainment.

Teach your child to knock the first glass over with a metal spoon.

Ask her whether she noticed a difference in the sound when she tapped the following glass.

Ask her to tap the other glasses and observe the difference in sound.

Interrogate her with, "What seems to be happening?"

Put her hypothesis to the test.

Alternative: Have your youngster listen intently while you tap a glass while she closes her eyes. Then you might ask her whether the tone she hears when you tap the other glass is higher or lower. Or, let

gently tapping the spoon on several glasses to make music.

The glasses are fragile, so make sure your toddler taps on them gently.

So, tell me, what can you do?

ENCOURAGE YOUR CHILD'S CREATIVE THINKING BY HAVING HIM FIND AMUSING USES FOR COMMON HOUSEHOLD GOODS.

Materials and Tools:

Your youngster may use a paper bag, a long scarf, a cardboard box, a balloon, a stick, a towel, a block, a cup, etc., to think creatively.

Instructions with necessary skills:

Put everything in a paper bag.

To encourage your child's creativity, choose an object and ask him to come up with a list of uses for it. If it's a scarf, he may wave it, wear it as a cloak, form a sling, tie it in a lump, use it as a necklace, roll it, fold it, wad it up, and toss it, among other possible uses.

Count up all the possible uses he can come up with. When he's done, tally up the number of applications he came up with!

Put the other things through the same process.

Combine two things and challenge him to think of new combinations of how they may be used.

Be careful, you won't want to be hurt!

SO, WHY AM I DIFFERENT?

Your kid sees you every day, but does she understand what she's seeing? Try out the game and find out for yourself!

Materials and Tools:

Items of apparel, jewelry, and other fashion items are scattered across the floor.

Instructions with necessary skills:

Make sure your kid can see you well by sitting on the floor with her.

You should assist her identify the pieces of clothes and accessories you are wearing by answering her questions.

Get her to shut her eyes and relax.

Unbutton your jumper, switch your watch to the other arm, take off your jewelry, flip your socks inside out, etc. to remove or alter only one item of clothing or accessory.

Challenge her to open her eyes and figure out what's distinctive about you.

Let her try on various styles as you try to identify the difference!

Alternately, you may dump all of your spare garments in the center of the room. In cases were

When the little one shuts her eyes, you switch out one of your garments for one of those on the stack. Attempt to elicit a reaction from her while hiding your differences.

Pay close attention to the quality of the apparel and jewels to ensure that she can handle them without harm.

A B C HOUR

This interactive game takes the traditional ABC learning process to a whole new level of pleasure for your youngster.

Materials and Tools:

Possession of a room, garden, or shop stuffed with plainly recognized objects

Instructions with necessary skills:

In a span of twenty-six days, have your kid focus on one letter of the alphabet. It makes no change what order you choose the letters in.

Give him several instances of the letter and the sound it creates. So, if he chooses the letter T, you would say "truck," "town," "toys," "tiger," "teacher," and so on.

Following some practice, have your youngster search the home, yard, or local shop for items that begin with the letter T. In your home, he could come across a toaster, train set, table, tea set, teaspoon, and so on.

Have fun exploring the day's letter in search of things that start with it. Have your youngster choose a different letter the next day.

You could also give him a pad of paper with the letter of the day written on it and ask him to draw pictures of anything he can think of that starts with that letter.

Carefully give him clues and keep repeating yourself to keep him from becoming upset.

noise he's making while looking for instances.

THE HUMBLE TOM
Laugh at his kooky fingers and thumbs while encouraging your youngster to act out human behavior.

Materials and Tools:

Different colored washable felt-tip pens Cuts of fabric in various sizes Tape

Instructions with necessary skills:

Draw eyes, ears, hair, a nose, and a mouth on your child's fingernails (with washable felt-tip pens, of course!) Have your youngster draw you, other family members, close friends, or other significant individuals in his or her life.

To make finger and thumb mittens for your kid, cut out little squares of cloth. Don't bother covering up your nail beds.

Wrap the cloth over his fingers and thumbs and tape them in place. Attempt to coordinate clothing with character features.

Try having your kid put on a Tom Thumb play using his fingers as the characters! If he needs help getting going, provide it.

Cut the fingers off of some old knit gloves for a variant. Get some gloves, some felt-tip pens, and your kid's fingers, and you've got a fun craft project. Give him another chance to perform a play.

You should check that the pens are harmless and can be cleaned.

SHOULD I BE...
If your kid could be anything, what would she do differently? Play this exciting game to find out!

Materials and Tools:

Periodicals or low-cost picture books Scissors

Instructions with necessary skills:

Make a collage with your kid using cutouts of interesting animals, creatures, things, locations, and anything else you may think of to encourage creative thinking.

Put the photos in an inverted stack.

Try asking her, "What would you do if you were a...?"
"

Let her continue the statement by flipping the first photo over.

Have her talk about what she would do if she were the image in the photo. Let her play the part if she wants to!

Keep exploring the remaining images.

Try your hand at it and see what the fuss is about!

Alternately, instead of showing her photographs of objects, put her in a position where she can learn about them.

questions such, "What would you do if you were lost?" are examples of hypothetical situations. Illnesses, maybe, or the feeling that you could. A fire, perhaps? Or maybe you've come upon a dollar. ," and so forth.

Make sure the scenarios aren't too terrifying, however.

IN A LINE

Introducing your kid to the power of series is a great way to help him get his life in order.

Materials and Tools:

Broken crayons can be arranged from smallest to largest; buttons can be arranged from shortest to longest; sticks can be arranged from darkest to lightest; cans can be arranged from smallest to largest; toys can be arranged from smallest to largest; dolls can be arranged from oldest to newest; clothes can be arranged from softest to stiffest; and so, on and so forth.

Instructions with necessary skills:

Collect a number of things that may be sequentially arranged.

Make a mountain out of them in the center of the floor or the table.

Put the stack in front of you and sit across from your kid.

Provide an example of a possible ordering, such as from shortest to tallest, smallest to biggest, darkest to lightest, or any other scheme that makes sense.

Instruct him to make a neat stack of everything by lining it up.

If he gets stuck, remind him of the organizing concept and assist him decide what to do next.

Collect a fresh set of materials and try again.

Optional twist: Instead of having your kid set up a sequential order, have him categorize the objects by color, shape, size, or any other characteristic.

Take care, you need to make sure they're safe to handle.

CONVERSION DAY

Your kid has probably mastered a ton of new, advanced skills recently. She may attempt to do them in reverse and see how much fun it is!

Materials and Tools:

Something like reversing the order in which you eat lunch, put on your clothing, or go for a stroll.

Instructions with necessary skills:

Pick up a game or chore that your kid knows how to perform backwards and they'll be set.

Advise her that, since it's Backwards Day, she must do all of her normal tasks in reverse order.

Get her dressed, feed her, walk her, etc., in reverse order!

Alternatively, you might celebrate "Opposite Day," in which everyone pretends to be one thing but really means the complete opposite.

You should double check that your youngster can complete the activities safely while wearing backwards.

PROPELLING A BALLOON

Balloons are great toys that can be used in a variety of games, helping your youngster develop important skills while having fun.

Materials and Tools:

It took 2 balloons to lift them off the ground or a tabletop.

Instructions with necessary skills:

Inflate a balloon for each person.

The balloons on the ground lay at one end of the room or yard.

Behind the balloons, go down on your hands and knees.

The time has come to launch your balloon across the room.

If you kick the balloon, bounce the balloon, knee the balloon, elbow the balloon, head-butt the balloon, etc., the first person to the other end gets to choose the next event.

Throw in a twist with a balloon relay competition. Blow up a bunch of balloons and set one on a disposable plastic plate. Make your way around the room on foot or two feet, but don't let the balloon pop! Repeat this process with the subsequent balloon until all of the balloons have been raced.

Be careful not to overinflate the balloons, since this might cause them to burst. You should play in an area that is free of obstructions.

PLANNING A LINE

Over the course of preschool, your child's creative abilities have blossomed. Design a Line is his chance to shine as an artist.

Materials and Tools:

White sketching paper in large sheets Felt-tipped pens

Instructions with necessary skills:

Come join your kid at the dinner table.

Set down some paper and felt-tip pens in front of him.

Make a line on the paper that is either straight, curved, wavy, or angular with one of the pens.

Get his opinion on the plan you've been working on.

Then, have him use his creativity to create an image based on the design you provide him.

When you're satisfied with the result, save the image and try again!

Draw shapes instead of lines and see if your kid can make up a picture from it.

Be careful to use non-hazardous felt-tip pens.

RUN AND HIDE IN THE WINTER

How soon can your kid slow down her motions before speeding them up again? Read Freeze and Flee to find out!

Materials and Tools:

Extensive Room

Instructions with necessary skills:

Get your kid to a safe, open area where he or she may run about and have fun.

The phrase "Flee!"

Your kid should be running around as quickly as she can.

As soon as the word "Freeze!" is spoken, everyone must stop moving.

She has to halt right this minute and remain motionless.

Insist on yelling "Flee!"

The phrases "Stop!

at least till she's worn out.

Alternately, you may yell out instructions like "Jump!

" "Dance!

" "Walk!

" "Crawl!

," and so forth.

It's important to keep your kid safe when they're playing, so make sure the environment is free of any obstacles.

HIDDEN PHOTO

If your kid enjoys doodling, he'll be thrilled to find hidden doodles in your work.

Materials and Tools:

Crayons (white and other colors) White paper

Instructions with necessary skills:

Use a white pastel on white paper to create an illustration. Your kid should not view your drawings.

Get him a chair and put the paper on the table in front of him.

Show him the hidden image on the paper and hand him the crayons.

With the help of the colored crayons, he must cover the paper and figure out how to disclose the image below. The other crayons will not be able to cover up the white crayon artwork, revealing the hidden image. Drop some hints if they're needed.

Then have him sketch you a picture of something you shouldn't see.

Use the Crayola Changeable felt-tip markers, which come with both an invisible marking pen and a variety of colored pens that disclose the invisible marks, for a variant on this activity.

Avoid your youngster becoming frustrated by having to constantly start again on huge pieces of paper by cutting them into smaller ones.

A SET OF BOWLING CUBS

An uncomplicated game of Bowling Boxes will help your kid work on his or her bowling arm.

Materials and Tools:

Supplies: a rubber ball of around medium size, a taped-together stack of six to eight empty cereal boxes, a surface that is not carpet

Instructions with necessary skills:

Gather up a number of cereal boxes, then tape the lids shut.

Arrange the cartons in a bowling pin-like triangle at one end of the room where there is no carpeting.

Send your kid over there and hand her the ball.

Tell her to roll the ball towards the cereal boxes in an attempt to knock them over.

Have her attempt again and again by rolling the ball back to her until all the boxes have been smashed.

Set up the boxes once again and play until she loses interest.

As an alternative, have your kiddo take a step backwards before each new game. Or, arrange the boxes such that the impact with the first one causes the others to fall.

Warning: Get rid of any breakables and become her near to the boxes the first time so she doesn't get irritated.

SPACE ANIMALS

An overcast day is ideal for this activity. Be wary of the huge, fluffy Cloud Creatures!

Materials and Tools:

Blanketing clouds

Instructions with necessary skills:

On a gloomy day, take your blanket outdoors and relax on the grass.

Lay side by side and observe the sky together.

Talk to your kid about what he or she sees in the sky.

Please describe what you saw to him.

Make up dramatic tales about the clouds and take it in turns telling them.

Make it a little different by asking your kid to draw clouds that resemble the cloud people. Ask him to come up with some fictitious tales to accompany them.

Warning: Wrap yourself warm if it's chilly, and don't forget the goggles if you need them. Don't stare straight at the sun; it might damage your eyes!

BREAK OUT INTO DANCE

Dancing is simple for your kid as long as she can utilize her complete body, but what if she can't?

Materials and Tools:

Playing a CD or cassette of dance music

Instructions with necessary skills:

Put in some disco tunes on a cassette or CD and get ready to dance!

Just turn on some tunes and feel the beat.

You may encourage your kid to move to the beat by telling her she can, but only if she uses one body part at a time.

Pick the part of her body you want to look at, such her finger, hand, knee, face, shoulder, leg, toe, and so on. Tell her to dance exclusively with that area of her body to the beat.

Have her dance in a variety of ways and touch various areas of her body as the song progresses.

Alternately, dance as a group and take turns naming different body parts to move.

Take care not to run into anything, and clear the space before proceeding.

DARK ENDING

Instead of tagging a person, how about you tag their shadow?

Materials and Tools:

It's a beautiful day outside

Instructions with necessary skills:

Find your shadows by venturing outside on a bright day.

When you and your partner have located your shadows, you may play a game of tag in which you attempt to walk on each other's shadows while avoiding having you .

She's the one that gets trodden on every time!

Alternately, position yourself such that your shadow falls onto a wall. The next time your kid is bored, hand her a ball and tell her to see if she can get your shadow. Never let it get too simple by not stopping to rest!

Be careful that your youngster doesn't hurt himself or herself by running into anything.

WARM WELCOME CARDS

Instruct your kid to talk about how he feels and how others make them feel.

Materials and Tools:

Envelopes, colored markers, and felt-tip pens on construction paper.

Instructions with necessary skills:

Share the joy of a birthday, healing from an illness, a new house, or other happy event with your kid by telling them about a relative or acquaintance.

Create a greeting card by folding a piece of construction paper in half, then in quarters.

Your youngster should design an image on the front that represents how they feel about it. To illustrate illness, one can depict a sick person lying in bed with a thermometer in his mouth.

Sayings like "Get well soon" or "I miss you" or anything else he wishes to convey might be written within the card.

To send the greeting card, just drop it in an envelope.

Alternate version: Motivate your kid to send greeting cards whenever they want. It's possible for him to convey sentiments like "I like you" and "You're the finest! "

Watch out! Teach your kid how to find the correct words to express how they feel.

THERE ARE THREE THINGS TO CONSIDER.

The number three is associated by some with a triumvirate of good fortune. Play a round of this exciting three-player game with your kid.

Materials and Tools:

Books with many illustrations Scissors Tiny envelopes Paper and felt-tip pens (optional)

Instructions with necessary skills:

Look through magazines for photographs of groups of three, such as ingredients for a pizza, parts of an outfit, facial traits, family members, and so on.

Remove the objects and sort them into threes after cutting them out.

Fold the groups into envelopes and place them on a table.

Ask your kid to choose an envelope, take out a photo, and describe it.

Inquire as to the identity of the other two images included in the envelope from her.

Instruct her to take down yet another image.

Examine the parallels between the two images and talk about them.

See if she can predict what the following image will be.

Get her to take down the last photo.

Have her explain the relationship between the three pieces.

Take the remaining envelopes and do it again.

Allow your youngster to take turns gathering three objects and guessing your reasoning behind their selection.

Take cautious that she doesn't cut herself with the scissors.

WHAT A MAGICAL IMAGE

See the miracle in your kid's eyes as he creates drawings emerge out of thin air!

Materials and Tools:

A paper bag a leaf, a doily, a credit card, an etched image, a stencil, a thin necklace, a coin, etc. They are all flat and have raised patterns that will show through the paper when rubbed with a crayon

Instructions with necessary skills:

Have fun with your kid by collecting objects he or she can rub together to make a pattern.

You should hide them in a paper bag from him.

Set the bag down on the table in front of you along with some white paper and crayons.

Give your kid a part of paper and tell him to shut his eyes while you slide anything beneath it.

Just give him a crayon and tell him to rub the paper until an image emerges.

Take away the paper and check whether he was accurate about the item's identity.

Iterate until all remaining items are dealt with.

Alternate version: Send your kid on a treasure hunt for things around the home that could

create enchanted images. Give them all a try, and then explain why some are successful while others are not.

Take care to just use non-hazardous materials, and choose for bigger crayons if you need them for simpler handling.

MEET AND GREET: A GOOD TIME

Your child's grasping and releasing abilities are highly developed at this point. But can she use tongs to take up objects?

Materials and Tools:

Pickup targets like a scrap of paper, a toy, a cracker, a pea, a necklace, a sandwich, and so on A large bowl Tongs for picking up targets off the floor or table

Instructions with necessary skills:

Gather a variety of little objects that will be difficult for your youngster to pick up with tongs but not impossible.

Place the things between you and her while you sit on the floor or at a table across from her.

Put them in instruction of easiest to most difficult to take up.

Placing the bowl where your kid can easily get to it is a great start.

Just hand her a set of tongs and see how she does.

Tell her to use the tongs to pick up the first thing and put it in the bowl.

Tell her to keep going until she has successfully gathered everything and deposited it in the bowl.

Change it up by instructing your youngster to use her toes as tongs.

Take care that the tongs are not too difficult to hold and don't have any jagged edges.

DRIVE, DRIVE, AND PLAY

Kids of all eternities and stages of development might find interesting challenges in playing with play dough. Some advice for parents of preschoolers is provided below.

Materials and Tools:

Kitchen implements such a big spoon, fork, dull knife, tiny bowl, garlic press, skewer, cookie cutter, cup, and so on Play dough, baker's clay, or any dough like material Table

Instructions with necessary skills:

Toy or baker's clay may be made at home or purchased elsewhere.

Prepare a workspace for the dough and the necessary equipment.

Your kid can make anything he wants out of the dough with the tools you provide.

If he's having problems getting going, offer him some suggestions like different kinds of food, animals, people, clothes, toys, etc.

Alternately, once your kid is done, bake the dough for two or three hours at 250 degrees Fahrenheit to harden it, and then let him paint it.

Warning: Make sure your kid knows how to handle cutlery properly.

CHANGE THE ORDER OF THE BEDS

Play a game of "guess the difference" by rearranging your kid's bedroom furniture.

Materials and Tools:

The sleeping quarters of your offspring

Instructions with necessary skills:

Give your kiddo a chance to take stock of what she has going on in there.

Then, have her go outside and shut the door behind her.

Put a cushion on top of the spread, flip the clock around, put her shoes on the hook normally used for her jacket, and so on while she's out of the house.

Invite her back in so she may look around.

Try inquiring as to whether or not she can identify the changes made to her quarters.

After she's finished noting the changes, give her a chance to help you rearrange her space.

Move the game to a new location in the home for some variety.

When it's her time to rearrange the furniture, take precautions to ensure that she stays away from any sharp or heavy things.

EXPRESS YOUR EMOTIONS

Sometimes kids just don't know how to put their sentiments into words. Here's a strategy for getting your kid to recognize and articulate his emotions.

Materials and Tools:

You may use Scissors to cut out pictures of people sobbing, smiling, furious, scared, etc. from magazines and cheap picture books.

Instructions with necessary skills:

Emotional facial expressions cut off.

Talk about how the fonts are feeling and why they are acting that way with your kid.

Make a pile with the photographs upside down.

Don't look as your kid flips the image over.

Get him to express the feeling via non-verbal means.

It's up to you to identify what feeling he's attempting to convey.

Immediately after making the right guess, you should exchange roles.

Flip the photographs over and act out your feelings in turn.

Alternative: use just your hands to convey feelings.

Caution: Choose feelings that are age-appropriate for your youngster.

SOMETHING ALTERNATIVE

Your child's cognitive growth will be aided by learning to categorize objects. Allow her plenty of time to practice classifying and dividing.

Materials and Tools:

Table made from a cupcake pan or egg carton filled with 6-8 containers of various little objects to sort (buttons, cereal, beads, beans, coins, raisins, and so on).

Instructions with necessary skills:

Put the can or box down on the table.

Make a pile of the little things next to the container.

Position your youngster near the materials by having them sit at a table.

Give her a few items and tell her to put one of them in each cup.

Then, have her choose another item and determine whether it should go in the same cup or if it requires a separate one.

Share your thoughts on the similarities and differences you see between the things with her.

Request that she keeps on organizing the remainder of the stuff.

Ask her to tally up the contents of each cup to determine which one holds the most.

When taking your kid shopping, try dividing the groceries into cold, hot, meat, veggies, boxes, bags, snacks, and health categories.

supplies, such as sustenance and the like. She'll appreciate hearing your thoughts on the similarities and differences you see between the things.

Take care that your youngster doesn't ingest any of the inedible tiny objects.

FICTION DRAMA

Have your youngster perform his favorite stories for you.

Materials and Tools:

Books for children's reading comfort items (a towel or sheet, a floor chair)

Instructions with necessary skills:

Select some of your child's favorite picture books for him to act out.

The floor should be covered with a big sheet or towel to serve as a stage.

Calmly read the narrative while sitting in a chair.

Put your kid in the spotlight in the center of the stage and have him or her performance out the story as you read it.

Make a video of the presentation and show it to him later as an alternative.

Take care that none of the scenarios you're planning to carry out are really harmful. Take your time reading aloud and provide your youngster any help they may need to get started.

TOOTHPICK-TURES

Various objects may be used by your youngster to create artwork. And only using toothpicks, see what he creates!

Materials and Tools:

Toothpicks, both plain and colorful; construction paper; table glue (optional).

Instructions with necessary skills:

Put a bowl of toothpicks on a table.

Put your kid in front of the table and have him use the toothpicks to create a picture.

If he's not sure where to begin, demonstrate how to manipulate the toothpicks into various forms (such as shapes, patterns, people, animals, and so on).

Once he's done, you may look at his photo and admire his work.

If he wants to get fancy, you could even have him glue his toothpick-true on a piece of construction paper.

Another option is to provide play dough and let him use it to cement the toothpick connections.

Warn him to use caution around the toothpicks since their points are sharp.

ADMIT IT

Have some laughs by switching around different facial features to create zany characters, and then challenge your youngster to put the faces back together again.

Materials and Tools:

Magazines with huge photographs of faces Scissors Glue or tape Construction paper

Instructions with necessary skills:

Large magazine cutouts of faces were used.

Remove the facial features by cutting off the eyes, noses, and mouths.

Put the remaining face features on scraps of paper using glue or tape.

Then, proceed to give each face the incorrect eyes, noses, and mouths.

Show your kid your silly expressions!

Inquire of her whether she can identify the facial features.

Tell her to shuffle the facial characteristics around until they look like they did before.

A little glue can restore the faces to their full glory.

Allow your youngster to take part in picking and rearranging the facial features.

Use caution while working with scissors.

STRANGE LETTERS

Your kid determination has a bang using his or her creativity to transform the letters of the alphabet into fantastical scenes.

Materials and Tools:

The table pad sketching paper the felt-tip pens or crayons

Instructions with necessary skills:

Have a seat at the bench and chat with your kid.

Just get her to name a letter of the alphabet.

Include the communication in the center of the sheet, written in big font.

Toss the sheet of paper over to her and tell her to draw something amusing using the letter as a template.

Change the letter you're working with.

Alternately, have your kid choose a number or symbol and draw a silly image out of it.

Make sure the communication is large enough to accommodate your kid's imagination.

FEET AND HANDS

If your kid knows how to differentiate her hands from her feet, then she should be able to recognize her handprints from her footprints. In other words, she'll have a great time on the Hands and Feet route!

Materials and Tools:

The materials you'll need are: construction paper, a felt-tip pen, scissors, and double-sided tape.

Instructions with necessary skills:

Your child's hands and feet should be traced on a piece of construction paper using a felt-tip pen. In order to create handprints and footprints, cut out the outlines.

Produce several copies of the prints.

Stick double-sided tape to the prints' backs.

Put them on the ground in a straight line from one end to the other of the room.

Instruct your kid to put either her foot or hand on the original print. See that she chooses left or right as needed.

Make her walk the rest of the way, stopping at each set of footprints, until she reaches the finish line.

If you want to up the difficulty, spread the prints more apart.

Be wary that your toddler can access the prints in the first game.

CLOCKWORKS

You may try looking for a vintage clock or other mechanized gadget in the basement or attic. Learning the mechanism behind it will be a wonderful adventure for your kid.

Materials and Tools:

Devices that use moving parts and may be safely disassembled Floor or table

Instructions with necessary skills:

Try searching online for an antique clock, or visit your neighborhood thrift store to find one.

You may set it down on the floor or a table.

Instruct your little one to use a screwdriver and other basic instruments.

Inquire of him to disassemble the clock.

Get him to attempt to find out the solution. If help is needed, provide it.

Take apart the clock and explain its inner workings as you go.

Alternately, you may try reassembling the clock or giving your youngster another basic object to disassemble.

WARNING: He should use caution around any sharp objects.

A CALL TO COLOR

Your youngster is developing prewriting skills, language, and gestures to discover how symbols convey meaning. Coloring in will be a lot of fun for her!

Materials and Tools:

Large open space for playing Felt-tip pens or crayons (optional) One sheet of each color of construction paper (red, blue, yellow, and green)

Instructions with necessary skills:

Get out four separate pieces of colored paper, preferably red, blue, yellow, and green.

...or use white paper, felt-tip pens, or crayons to have your kid design them .

Seek out a big open space where your kid can run about.

Tell her that whenever she sees one of the colors you hold up, she has to do the corresponding action. If you show her a piece of red paper, she has to leap; if you show her a piece of blue paper, she has to run, and so on.

Put your kid smack in the midst of the play area.

Put up a piece of colored paper and have her do the corresponding motion.

Don't drop the shade on the floor. She must instantly begin doing that other thing.

Keep holding up different colors and switching up the motion until she gives up!

To make the game more difficult, try varying the number of colors and the number of objectives.

Please take it easy at initially to prevent your toddler from being overtired.

HEAR THE MUSIC

Listening to music as you create is a soothing experience. Alsu's not only fun, but it teaches your kid new things and encourages him to find his voice.

Materials and Tools:

Several cassettes of different genres of prerecorded music Drawing pad Felt-tip pens or crayons

Instructions with necessary skills:

Various genres of music, including classical, country, western, pop, rock, hip-hop, children, and so on, should be recorded into tape. Set the regulator for one to three minutes for each style.

Give your youngster some sketching paper and either felt-tip pens or crayons to express their creativity.

Put on some tunes and tell him to sketch whatever comes to mind.

Tell your youngster to flip the page whenever the music does, and to start a new sketch with each new piece of music.

To complete the cassette, just keep repeating.

Toss his images about and replay the video. Try playing it again and seeing if he can identify the associated images and genres of music.

Let your kid explain how he felt listening to various kinds of music.

Create a tape containing non-musical sounds, such as the sound of an engine running, water flowing, birds tweeting, and so on as an alternative. Try out the aforementioned procedure once again and observe your kid's inventiveness.

Warning: avoid anything that can be overly gloomy or confusing for the listeners.

HAVING FUN ON THE EDGE

Here's a fun method for your kid to engage in imaginative play with both his or her body and his or her thoughts!

Materials and Tools:

Rope length of 5 feet, for a very large region

Instructions with necessary skills:

Find a big open space where your kid can run about in safety.

Place the rope in a straight line with plenty of space on each side.

Put your kid at the beginning of the rope's loop.

Tell her she must cross the walkway as if it were made of ice. Tell her to use an ice-appropriate gait.

Have her go back down the same route, this time envisioning it to be made of burning coals, when she reaches the opposite side.

Keep picturing different floors for her to walk on, and have her come up with a unique gait for each one. The list strength goes on and on, but some examples are as follows: lush grass, thick sand, slimy muck, sharp pine needles, deep snow, sticky glue, etc.

Take it one step further by instructing your youngster to go barefoot and blindfolded down the trail.

Be careful that your youngster doesn't hurt himself or herself by running into anything.

THEN WHAT WILL HAPPEN?

Playing What Happens Next? with your kid is a great way to teach him or her to think ahead and make educated guesses.

Materials and Tools:

Magazine or cheap picture book with plenty of photographs Cozy chair

Instructions with necessary skills:

Have your youngster join you in a comfy chair, so that you can both read the magazine.

Flip to the first photo that catches your eye.

Confer with him about the events shown.

Prompt him to think about the possible outcomes.

After you've finished discussing those images, flip the page to see more.

Alternatively, you may read a picture book to your youngster and then pose the question, "What do you think will happen next?"

as you prepare to flip the page.

Take care that the magazine doesn't include any graphic or upsetting photos.

THE FLEA CIRCUS

Visit the Flea Circus for a fun game that will help your kid think outside the box.

Materials and Tools:

Materials Needed: Imaginary Fleas, a Table, or the Floor, Construction Paper, Scissors, and Felt-Tip Pens

Instructions with necessary skills:

Make a three-ring circus by slicing three huge circles from construction paper.

Arrange the circles next to one another on a flat surface.

Take a seat with your little one so that you're both seeing at the ringside action.

Tell him it's a flea circus, and the acts are so little they're hardly visible.

Using your finger to point out the many flea behaviors is a great way to encourage your child's creativity. Here comes the flea lion, and there's the flea tamer over there," you can add. Get ready to see the flea lion splat through the hoops! Oh, my goodness, he finally made it! For being so cooperative, the flea tamer is rewarding the lion with a treat. Look! The flea circus clowns have arrived! Check out that dolt performing somersaults! You may help your youngster visualize the performances by describing them while moving your finger.

Get him to tell you about the other performers at the flea circus as he points them out with his finger.

Alternately, you may stage other tiny situations and have your youngster visualize them.

Take care, and if your youngster seems irritated or confused, just remind him that it's all pretend.

PUT ON A SHOW

Is your kid able to communicate in ways outside words? To have some fun, play Act It Out!

Materials and Tools:

Coloring books

Instructions with necessary skills:

Make it a family action by letting your kid pick out a picture book to act out. Recommend that you have her keep her choice a secret.

Just wait for her to finish the narrative and then ask her to summarize it silently. Without using any words, she must play out the scenario for you, and you must decipher her intentions.

Say the terms that describe your child's actions while she plays out the narrative.

Read the book together afterward and compare notes on how well you guessed.

You may also encourage your kid to play out other scenarios, such as her day at preschool, a scene from a movie she's watched, a family tale, and so on.

It's important that your kid select a tale she's already read, so she won't be confused about what to perform in the play.

STIRRED TOGETHER

To test your child's growing capacity for reasoning, have him or her play a round of All Mixed Up.

Materials and Tools:

a collection of complementary objects, such those found in a sandwich, an outfit, a puzzle, etc.

Instructions with necessary skills:

Amass the gear you'll need for the task at hand.

Get started with the task at hand, but do something incorrectly to see whether your youngster will catch on. You might use this phrase while making a peanut butter and jelly sandwich: "First put the bread on the peanut butter."

He has to tell her, "That's a mess!"

Keep chipping away at it, learning from your successes and your failures. It's good to have someone there to help you out when you goof.

Allow your toddler to try his hand at causing confusion and see if you can spot him in the act.

Alternate version: Confuse the tale you're telling. Have your youngster explain the problem and check whether he can still recall the plot.

Parents must be on the lookout for signs of confusion or frustration and respond accordingly by providing enough hints and reassurance.

HOP IN THE DARK

Give your kid the gift of newfound perspective by taking her on a Blind Walk.

Materials and Tools:

Covering Your Eyes in the Wild (optional)

Instructions with necessary skills:

Look for a park or other natural spot to wander in.

Instruct your little kid to shut her eyes and put her confidence in you. If she's game, a blindfold is your best bet.

Make her walk with you by holding your hand.

Invite her to part her impressions of the sounds, scents, and touches she is experiencing.

Have her touch things along the way, such trees, rocks, flowers, etc.

Ask her to explain how she feels and make an educated estimate as to what that feeling may be. Let her know if she's correct!

Keep on strolling, making sure your kid is OK, and let her take in everything around her without using her eyes.

The Blind Walk may be modified by letting a young kid take the lead; just make sure she knows to watch out for any hazards.

Be wary of anything that might injure or frighten her, such as low-hanging branches, squished feet, sharp pebbles, unexpected animals, and so on.

GAS BALLOON VOLLEY

Put your child's energy to good use by having him or her bat around a balloon that keeps dropping to the floor.

Materials and Tools:

Blown-up balloons huge playground equipment

Instructions with necessary skills:

Locate a large, open area where you won't have to worry about hitting anything as you bat a balloon about.

Bounce the balloon off the ceiling and toward your kid.

Have your kid smack the falling balloon back up toward you as it floats to the ground.

Bat the balloon back and forth to keep it aloft for as long as possible.

The rules may be changed by giving each player a balloon and challenging them to keep it aloft for as long as possible.

It's important to check the surroundings to make sure you won't run into anything.

BAGS OF FEELS

Children in the preschool years learn mostly via sensory experiences. Playing Feely Bags with your youngster may aid in the development of his or her tactile sense.

Materials and Tools:

a floor or table and six or eight paper bags filled with various textures, such as a sponge, ball of clay, handful of rubber bands, sheet of sandpaper, sticky sweets, glob of Slime, a package bow, a flower, etc.

Instructions with necessary skills:

Fold the top of each paper bag and place the items inside.

Get the bags out and put them in the middle of the room between you and the kid.

I want him to choose a bag, open the lid, and reach in blindly.

When he touches something, instead of asking him to identify it, have him describe how it feels.

Just wait for him to finish describing it and then take a go at it yourself.

Put your guess to the test by having your kid get the item from the bag.

Keep having fun with the other bags.

An alternative is to have your kid gather objects for you to touch and explain so you can play "Guess Who?" with him.

Carefully choose just the ones that won't pose any danger when handled.

Your child's fingers are learning to follow her lead more and more. She may practice her motor skills with a round of Finger Golf and have a great time.

Materials and Tools:

Park with plenty of room to run around 6 sheets of green construction paper Scissors Black felt-tip pen Double-stick tape

Instructions with necessary skills:

Get out into a big open space.

Cut out circular shapes from green construction paper to use as golf greens.

Mark a hole in the center of each green, three inches in diameter, and label it with a number.

Spread the greens out throughout the room, a few feet apart in sequential sequence.

Use double-sided tape to fasten the grass to the ground.

Apply double-sided tape over each opening to prevent balls from falling through.

The first hole is a few feet away, so set up your golf or ping pong balls there.

Players take turns directing a set of balls toward a target by batting at them with their fingers.

the opening tee off.

You can get the ball into the hole faster if you take turns pushing it.

Go back and do the same thing with the other voids.

Alternately, you might create a miniature golf course in the backyard for your little one to enjoy while working on his or her motor skills. Make your challenging holes with plastic golf clubs and balls.

Warning: Flicking your finger too forcefully might cause pain.

"I CAN!

Make a "I CAN!" sign to help your kid see everything he's capable of.

You can see his progress every week on the chart.

Materials and Tools:

Stickers or stars Poster board and a ruler

Instructions with necessary skills:

To create the graph, just draw grid lines on a sheet of poster board.

Type "I CAN!"

at the very top.

Include things like "Brush my teeth," "Get myself dressed," "Feed the dog," and so on along the left side of the page to show how much your youngster has accomplished.

Add an item to the list of things your kid has done every week. It's important to remind your youngster of his accomplishments every so often.

Alternate version: make a list of the things you want your kid to learn or do in the future and then guide him in his efforts to achieve those things. As he achieves new goals, keep a running tally of his "I CAN! " Chart.

Warning: Look at even the smallest accomplishments each week that your youngster has made. As the saying goes, "the journey of a thousand miles starts with one step."

FORGE A LINKAGE

Create a colorful paper chain with your kid to mark the days till a big occasion!

Materials and Tools:

Supplies: colored construction paper, cut into 1-by-4-inch strips Scissors Felt-tip pens or stickers Calendar Tape or glue

Instructions with necessary skills:

Pick out an important day on the calendar, like a holiday or your kid's birthday.

The days before the big event will fly by in no time if you help your youngster keep track of them.

Make as many strips as indicated. Don't forget to include a holiday-themed one!

Circle the date on the special-occasion strip, and then sequentially number the remaining strips starting with 1.

Using the special-occasion strip as a model, demonstrate to your youngster how to build chain links by first forming a ring with the strip and then joining the ends of the ring using glue or tape.

Using the 1 marked strip, thread it through the holiday connector and secure the ends with tape.

Attach the next numbered strips in the same fashion.

Each day, have your youngster cut the strip in half and remove the link with the highest number. He can easily keep track of how many days are left till the show.

event!

Making a necklace of treats and letting your kid consume one each day is a fun variation.

Tape, not glue, will make quick work of this. Avoid cutting your kid or other people's children accidentally.

DRESS LIKE A SUPERHERO

Towels and safety pins may transform even the most average youngster into a superhero.

Materials and Tools:

What You Need: A Colorful Towel or Piece of Fabric to Make a Cape Two Safety Pins Socks, Tights, a Paper Crown, a Mask, Gloves, And a T-Shirt with An Emblem (optional)

Instructions with necessary skills:

Collect the supplies you'll need to create your kid's superhero outfit.

Use safety pins to fasten a towel or cape to the back of her clothing.

Give her the freedom to accessorize whatever she sees fit.

Instruct her to create a name for her new superhero.

Interrogate her about her extraordinary abilities and find out what she can accomplish that no one else can!

Put her in charge of saving the day!

Make a cardboard fort and pretend to be a superhero within.

Caution: Reassure your youngster that it's only a game and to avoid taking any chances.

CUT OFF YOUR HANDS!

Give your kid a challenge where she can't use her hands and see how she adapts!

Materials and Tools:

tools for performing a certain activity, such as a washcloth to clean her face, a sock to place on her foot, a meal to eat, and so on.

Instructions with necessary skills:

Select a job that will stretch your kid while still being within her capabilities and that she can do without using her hands.

Don't try to tell her how to do the assignment. The teeth, the feet, the skull, and so on are all fair game.

Keep a near eye on her while she works through the puzzles, and give her praise when she does so.

After she's done, have her clap and say, "Look, Mom, no hands!"

The youngster may also place her arms behind her back for this variation. Put your arms through the slots between her padded arms and sit behind her. Tell her what to do and take control of her hands as she does it!

Make sure it's not too challenging, and keep an eye out that she doesn't do anything risky to get the job done.

NOISEMAKER

Your youngster will have a great time trying to predict your noises and will develop a liking for making sounds.

Materials and Tools:

Table or floor Blindfold (optional) Tape recorder and tape (optional) Noise-producing devices such a doorbell, cat, water faucet, vacuum cleaner, telephone, typewriter, train, automobile engine, flushing toilet, and so on Quiet room

Instructions with necessary skills:

Create a list of several objects your kid is already acquainted with that make noise. Before you begin the game, you may also wish to tape a variety of noises.

Place your kid in a quiet room with you, and have him sit at a table or on the floor to listen. Have him shut his eyes or blindfold himself so he can't see what happens.

Make a noise like one of the things you have written down.

To help your kiddo learn to guess, ask him or her to help. If you need to, provide some pointers.

Iterate with the remaining noises.

Alternately, you may have your youngster match the noises to the images you've cut out and laid out on the floor or table. You might even switch roles and have him make noises for you to identify.

Care should be taken to prevent your youngster from being startled or having his hearing damaged by excessively loud noises.

OUTLINE OF THE SUBJECT

Do you know whether your kid can identify anything by its silhouette? Play this exciting game to find out!

Materials and Tools:

Construction or drawing paper Fine felt-tip pen Paper bag Assorted shaped items, such as a cookie cutter, fork, ball, action figure, shoe, toy vehicle, pencil, toothbrush, and so on

Instructions with necessary skills:

Pick out a number of objects with clean contours.

Put each object on its piece of paper, and then trace its contour using a fine-tipped felt-tip pen.

Collect the templates, and then put them all in a paper bag.

Ping your kid to come in here.

Let her try to guess what it is by looking at the first outline. When in doubt, provide clues.

When her estimate is accurate, take the object out of the bag and set it where the outline is supposed to go.

And so on for the break of the things.

Alternatively, when your kid has guessed the object, she may fill in the outline with her drawings of the finer characteristics. Or, have your kid create silhouettes and try to guess what they are.

Objects should be safe to handle, so proceed with caution.

HEAD AS FLAT AS A PAPER BAG

Your kid will have an explosion exploring the world via a unique perspective, thanks to the paper bag that's been placed over his head.

Materials and Tools:

Supplies to decorate the paper bag large paper bag Table Felt-tip pens, crayons, stickers, etc.

Instructions with necessary skills:

Place a paper bag flat, flap side down, on the table.

Make a human head, monster head, robot head, or anything else your kid may think of by having them paint and decorate a bag.

Make slits for your eyes in the bag.

Give your kid some time to explore the home or yard while wearing the bag over his head and peering through the holes.

Prod him with the question of what it's like to have a paper bag for a skull.

To up the difficulty level, try putting the bag over your kid's head without cutting any eyeholes. Keep an eye on him as he moves about, since he can only see what's underneath him.

Keep your kid under careful supervision while he explores the home and yard, and remove any potential hazards.

GRAB THEM

Give your kid the chance to practice her fine motor skills in a pleasant way with this activity.

Materials and Tools:

Plastic drinking straws Bare floor or table

Instructions with necessary skills:

Please have a seat on the table or the bare floor.

Have your kid stand in the center of the floor or table with a bunch of drinking straws held vertically above him or her.

Just let her drop the straws and see where they land.

Remove one grass at a time from the tangled pile without touching the other straws.

If a player pulls a straw from the pile without disturbing the others, she gets to retain the straw.

If you move or disrupt another straw, your turn is finished and you must return the straw to the pile.

Don't stop the music till everyone has a straw.

Playing using toothpicks adds a new level of difficulty to the game.

Toothpicks are sharp; use caution to avoid injury.

PURELY SIMON SAYS

You may play this fun game with your preschooler by making the rules easier.

Materials and Tools:

spacious lawn ideal for games

Instructions with necessary skills:

Put yourself in front of your kid.

When you say, "Simon says," your kid should do anything you tell them to do with their body. Be sure to show the correct motion when you issue the order.

Tell your kid that he should only do what you say if you preface it with "Simon says."

After the third or fourth instruction, you may attempt to deceive him by skipping the "Simon says" part. In this case, the fact that you didn't state "Simon says" should be enough for him to deny doing the exercise.

If his understanding is right, play on.

Let him play Simon for a while if he gets it incorrect.

Another option is to omit the "Simon Says" part of the game and instead only provide orders. Give your youngster an order and then do something completely different to see whether he notices.

Be cautious and go at a modest speed at first so that your youngster can understand the instructions without becoming irritated.

DISCUSSION PERIOD

Conversation is what happens when two individuals take it in turns chatting to one another. It's called Talking Time when two individuals are conversing at once.

Materials and Tools:

Regardless matter where you put them, you can't miss these two visually rich periodicals.

Instructions with necessary skills:

Split the magazine in half and give one to the kid.

Relax on the floor or at a table and flip through the magazines in secret.

Choose one image to discuss with your kid and choose one for yourself.

Prepare a thirty-second countdown clock.

The moment I say "Go," everyone start discussing their photos simultaneously.

Do your best to hear what the other person is saying while you both engage in conversation.

As soon as the buzzer sounds, please recount the other person's last words.

Put your face on display and see whether the other person understood you.

Another option is to tell tales that revolve around a certain theme. Methods 4-8 should be followed.

A word of warning: cut down on the time if your kid starts to become antsy.

GOLDEN MAP

Is your home a treasure hunt for your kid? There is hope if you have a treasure map.

Materials and Tools:

Craft paper and markers or candy as a reward

Instructions with necessary skills:

Create a floor plan of your home.

Have your kid have a look at the home plan and then use it to provide a tour around the residence.

Place some treats throughout the house and have your kids find them.

Just try giving your kid the map again and seeing if she can locate the hidden prize.

Instead of hiding anything, let your kid conceal it for you.

Be careful to stow the reward away somewhere secure.

YARN WORLD WIDE WEB

Take your kiddo on a whirlwind adventure as she follows the yarn web that circles her from head to toe and back again.

Materials and Tools:

Weaving with a rainbow of colors

Instructions with necessary skills:

Obtain a hank of brightly colored yarn.

The yarn may be wrapped around a doorknob at one end of the room to mark the starting point.

As you go one piece of furniture to another, loop the unraveling yarn around each one.

Locate a suitable trail terminus.

Your slight one will be enchanted by the web of yarn you've created outside the entrance.

Put your finger on the beginning and instruct her to ride the yarn all the way to its conclusion. Make her keep track of it as she goes.

Alternately, offer her a reward of some kind for reaching the conclusion.

Take care not to shawl the yarn over any fragile objects, such as lamps.

Chapter 11: Mindfulness for Kids: Easy & Fun Activities

Mindfulness for Kids is a great resource for parents who want to help their children become more mindful. mindfulness-based interventions have been shown to be real in improving children's mental health and cognitive development, and can be done on a family level. The goal of this guide is to provide you with the resources you need to start your own mindfulness intervention with your child, as well as insights on how to best use mindfulness for your child's benefit.

What is Mindfulness.

Mindfulness is a repetition of paying attention in a non-judgmental way. Mindfulness can be used in our personal, family, and professional lives. It helps us understand ourselves better, find peace in difficult times, and develop concentration and focus.

How Can Mindfulness Be Used in Your Child's Life

Mindfulness can help to recover the quality of our children's lives by teaching them to pay attention to their thoughts, feelings, and sensations. It also helps them become more aware of their own emotions and behavior. By using mindfulness in their everyday lives, we can help our children grow into healthy adults who are able to handle challenges effectively and build lasting relationships.

How to Start Mindfulness in Your Child's Life.

Mindfulness can be a countless way to improve your child's overall well-being. When you choose a time to start mindfulness, make sure it is suitable for your child. For example, if you want to start mindfulness during the morning or afternoon, choose a time when there is slight or no sound and they are quiet.

Be Mindful of Your Child's gestures and words

When you are mindful of your child's gestures and words, you will be able to understand their thoughts and feelings better. By being conscious of what your child is saying, you will be able to encourage them to communicate more freely with you and others.

Ask Your Child How Mindfulness is Helping Them

If your child has worry stating themselves verbally, try asking them how mindfulness is helping them express themselves more effectively. This will help them understand why mindfulness has been beneficial for them in the past and may help them learn new techniques for mindful living.

Tips for Mindfulness in Your Child's Life.

If you're looking to introduce mindfulness to your child, it's important to keep a practice home. Mindfulness can be an inordinate way to help them learn self-care and stress-relief skills. You can also start small by teaching your child how to use mindfulness in their everyday lives. For example, if you want them to be more mindful during dinner, have them sit down and eat in silence for a few minutes each time.

Set Limits on What Mindfulness Can Do for You

While mindfulness is great for reliever, it should never become an escape from reality. Try to limit the amount of time or space you allow yourself to be mindful. This will help your child stay focused on the present and develop healthy habits that will benefit them long term.

Let Mindfulness Play a Role in Your Child's Life

One of the most significant things you can do as a parent is let your child have their own space when it comes to practicing mindfulness. This means setting boundaries so that your child isn't overwhelmed with too much mindfulness at once and instead has time for themselves each day without worrying about what else they should be doing. By giving your child some control over their own life through this type of discipline, you can help them build healthy habits that will last into adulthood.

Mindfulness can be a great way to improve your child's life. By choosing a time and place to start mindfulness, you can help them be more mindful of their everyday gestures and words. In addition, by setting limits on what mindfulness can do for them, you can ensure that it remains an important part of their lives. Finally, through the use of helpful tips and practices, you can encourage your child to turn their attention inward and focus on the present moment.

Fun Mindfulness Activities for Kids

Mindfulness has become a popular way to help children cope with difficult situations. It's a great way to break through negative thinking and increase self-awareness. And it can be fun, too! Here are five mindfulness activities for kids that will help them connect with their own mind and body.

Get your children involved in mindfulness.

If you're look to get your children complicated in mindfulness, the first step is to get them started. This section will explore how to start Mindfulness in Your Home. We'll also recommend 30 activities for kids that can help them learn and practice mindfulness. Finally, we'll provide tips on how to use mindfulness technology with your children.

Mindfulness Activities for Kids

Once you understand how to start Mindfulness in Your Home, it's time to get creative and start teaching your little ones some fun mindfulness activities! Here are some recommended activities for kids:

1) Sit down with a book and focus on the cover or text

2) colonize a favorite toy with mindfulness

3) Take a break from tech-intensive tasks and scan the screen without an anxiety

4) Make an altar out of empty foam cups (or any other objects you like) and sit at the foot of it; spend five minutes every day there before going back to work

5) Draw attention away from negative thoughts by taking a deep breath or counting backward from 100

How to Mindfully Use Technology

Once your children have some basic skills in mindfulness, it's time to start using technology more mindfully. In this section, we'll explore how to use mindfulness technology in fun and effective ways. We'll also deliver tips on how to use mindfulness technology with your children.

Some ways you can use mindfulness technology with your children include:

1) adjustable screensavers that help them relax

2) apps that allow you to focus on nature or peaceful activities without distractions

3) games that keep kids entertained while they practice mindfulness

4) photos and videos that feature calming moments or scenes from nature

How to Connect with Mindfulness.

When you start a mindfulness session, be sure to establish some foundational principles. These principles will help your child connect with mind and body in a healthy way. For example, allow children to start the session by connecting with their own thoughts and feelings. This will help them develop self-awareness and begin to understand how they experience the world around them.

Connect with Your Own Mind

Once your child has connected with their own mind, it's time to explore what it feels like to connect with others. As they communicate with others in a mindful way, they will learn about communication skills and how to work together as a team.

Connect with Others

One of the greatest important things you can do when engaging in mindfulness is connect with others. By talking about what's going on in your mind and sharing any insights, you will help other people better understand mindfulness and themselves. Additionally, by teaching kids' mindfulness, you can introduce them to this valuable skill set early on in their lives.

How to Mindfully Use Technology.

One way to connect with mindfulness is through technology. For example, you can use your phone to read articles about mindfulness or take a guided meditation class. Or, you could use your phone to create a mindfulness "Calm Corner" where you can write down some thoughts or answer questions about mindfulness.

Mindful Technology Use

Another way to connect with mindfulness is through technology. You can use apps that help you focus and learn about mind-body problems, like Mindfulness Coach for iPhone or Mindfulness Meditation for Android. You can also use online tools that allow you to journal about your experiences with mindfulness, or find online courses that teach meditation and other mind-body techniques.

Use Technology to Connect with Others

You can also connect with others through technology. For example, you can join a mailing list or chat room where you can share your thoughts on mindful topics, or join a Facebook group where you can discuss the benefits of mindfully using technology in your everyday life. You could also sign up for email newsletters that send tips and insights on mindful topics daily (or fortnightly).

Use Technology to Mindfully Use Your Home

Finally, one way to connect with mindfulness is through our own home environment: by using our devices to read articles about mindful living, listen to music that inspires contemplation, watch videos about mindful living, or take up some calming exercises like yoga or meditation at home. Using our devices in a safe and fun way can help children develop an appreciation for their own attentions and the concentrations of others around them – something that will have ripple effects on their lives and relationships long after they leave school!

If you want to introduce your children to mindfulness, there are numerous ways to do so, there are many ways to do so. Starting with mindfulness activities for kids can help them develop their awareness and concentration skills. Mindfulness in public can provide opportunities for children to connect with others and learn about the benefits of mindfulness. As they use technology to connect with mindfulness, they can also use it as a way to mindfully use their home. Teachers can use technology to connect with their students through mindful mediation techniques. Lastly, parents should consider using technology to connect with their children through mindful technologies such as digital wellbeing tools and apps. Following these humble steps can assistance your children develop good habits that will last a lifetime.

CONCLUSION

We hope you enjoyed our book! Here, we discussed the idea of how play therapy activities can help parents and children bond and tackle any emotional stability issues. These doings can be done with broods of any ages, but take into account your child's age and the skills they may or may not currently have. If you're unsure what to do, find an experienced play therapist or counselor! These activities are a fantastic way to help your children build social and emotional skills while also engaging them.

We know that sometimes parents and children can be at odds, which can be very stressful for parents in particular. We want to be a reserve for families and want to help create a positive bonding experience for parents and children.

Made in the USA
Las Vegas, NV
04 July 2023